BURNING POISON

BURNING POISON

THE MURDER THAT ROCKED
GEORGIAN LIVERPOOL

GLENN CHANDLER

Lea Valley Press

Lea Valley Press
7, Tudor Road
Wheathampstead
Hertfordshire
AL4 8NW

email leavalleypress@yahoo.com

First published in 2000.
All rights reserved.
Copyright Glenn Chandler
ISBN 0 9538338 0 1

Cover: Burning Poison by Christopher J. Delaney.

Typeset in Galliard by NW.

Printed and bound by Gomer Press, Llandysul,
Wales.

A CIP catalogue record for this book is available from the
British Library.

For Dad, in memory

Contents

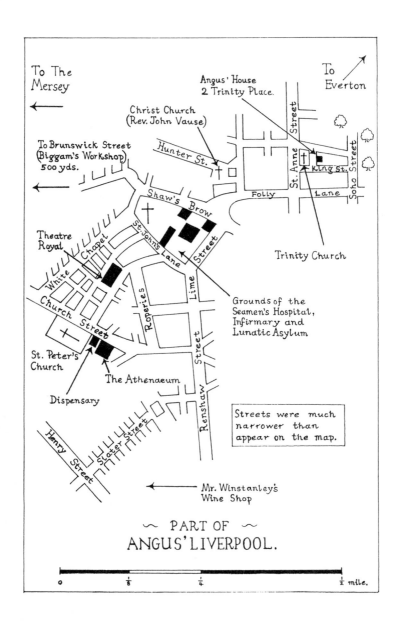

To The Mersey

To Everton

Angus' House
2 Trinity Place.

Christ Church
(Rev. John Vause)

To Brunswick Street
(Biggam's Workshop)
500 yds.

Hunter St.

St. Anne Street

King St.

Soho Street

Folly

Lane

Shaw's Brow

Theatre Royal

White

Chapel

St. John's Lane

Lime Street

Trinity Church

Roperies

Grounds of the
Seamen's Hospital,
Infirmary and
Lunatic Asylum

Church Street

St. Peter's Church

The Athenaeum

Renshaw Street

Dispensary

Streets were much
narrower than
appear on the map.

Slater Street

Henry Street

Mr. Winstanley's
Wine Shop

~ PART OF ~
ANGUS' LIVERPOOL.

0   ⅛   ¼   ½ mile.

FOREWORD

by

RICHARD WHITTINGTON-EGAN

Looking in this strange and fascinating book at the engraving of foursquare Trinity Church, and a somehow furtive-seeming Trinity Place, I am irresistibly reminded of the mezzotint.

The mezzotint, an engraving of an old English manor house by moonlight, is the centre-piece of a haunting tale in M.R. James' *Ghost Stories of an Antiquary*. Within the black frame borders of that picture eerie things happen. Where, on the lawn fronting the house, there is at first no-one, a dark, crawling figure appears - then disappears. A ground-floor window, previously shut, is now open. The 'thing' has got into the house. The picture changes again. Under scudding clouds and waning moon, a figure is once more to be seen upon the lawn, no longer crawling, but erect and striding away from the window, now closed again. The creature, skeletal, black drapery hanging down over its face, clasps tightly a child, whether dead or alive there is no sign to tell. The horrid scene fades. All lies quiet under the argent wash of moonbeams. But the picture has told its story. From the house represented, the last heir, it transpires, had mysteriously disappeared in infancy.

Reading here of this classic Liverpool mystery, so well and skilfully recounted by Glenn Chandler, I found myself unable to resist the impulse to turn and turn again to that engraving of Trinity Church and Place, and – to the mind's eye at least – it seemed to change, to become alive and peopled. Here, cloak flapping in the strong Mersey wind, comes the stern figure of Charles Angus, hurrying round the corner, a Scot who took the traditional Johnsonian high road to England and prosperity as a merchant. But who – or what – is this shrouded, muffled thing one seems to glimpse shuffling, sinister behind him? Has it not something of a death's head about it? Is this a portent of murder? And see there, a little nearer in the foreground, a young wife, scarcely more than a child herself, walks with her three children. She walks in the shadow of a coffin. Another figure, a young woman, small, sallow, plainish of countenance, is visible beside the churchyard wall. She, too, walks in a coffin's shade.

There is a kind of magic in the way that Glenn Chandler conjures a vanished world back to life. It is as if, gazing at an old sepia picture of a bird's-eye view of the city, one were to be handed a camcorder with an adjustable time-machine lens, and find oneself suddenly able to zoom right down into a scene which transforms itself from faded sepia into the vivid blue and white of a breeze-spiced living day in the old town : Georgian Liverpool.

I know the lineaments of old Liverpool well, having written books that mapped it, its quaint citizenry and sundry odd happenings in its chequered history. Having made also a profession of crime - by writing about it, that is - I have come to know quite a deal concerning criminous Liverpudlians, ancient and modern. I was even on nodding terms with Charles Angus, but Glenn Chandler's synchronously wide-sweeping and deep-dredging study of the case, and of the early nineteenth-century Liverpool against which it was set, has revealed to me much on both scores. Particularly impressive is the author's delving into the historico-medical context. In Gilbertian terms, one must say of his assessment of the doctors' evidence that it is the very model of a medical analysis.

Patently, Glenn Chandler belongs to the get-up-and-get-out-and-get-under school of practical investigators. He does not restrict his research to the raking of libraries, the culling of crumbling documents; he has actually journeyed to all relevant loci, ransacked family memories, and is thus able to supplement passive historic data with the results of active contemporary comparison. One would scarcely have thought it possible to have unearthed after the passage of virtually two hundred years anything approaching what he has salvaged from the rust and dust, the mildew and moths of time. In this sensitive reconstruction, Glenn Chandler has, I believe, provided the most likely answer to an enigma which has eluded and defied resolution for two centuries. He has now, in this book, embalmed for all time everything that we can hope to know about as mysterious an affair and as weird and wonderful a character as you are likely to meet in several lifetimes.

INTRODUCTION

Turn right outside Lime Street Station in Liverpool, walk northwards past the magnificent edifice of St George's Hall, strike off at an oblique angle, and you come to a busy traffic intersection which marks the southern end of St Anne Street. Across the lanes of traffic is a small embankment planted with trees, and just beyond that a low modern block of red brick dwellings called Trinity Walk. This marks the site of Trinity Church, which was swept away in the 'sixties, and Trinity Place, a neat respectable row of houses which used to run along the east side of the churchyard.

In the year 1808, Number Two Trinity Place was the residence of Mr Charles Angus, a Liverpool merchant. Around the house and its occupants an almost unfathomable haze of mystery exists. The story is a grim one, involving murder, illegal abortion, deadly poison, perjury and malice. Its component parts are a bizarre mixture. A ghastly surgical instrument with an equally ghastly catalogue of purposes. A baby that disappears in the middle of a crisp March morning. A corpse with a hole in its stomach. Conflicting medical evidence in a trial for murder that was to become a *cause célèbre*. Above all, it is a tantalising puzzle, set in a dark corner of Georgian England against a backdrop of Liverpool prosperity and the slave trade.

It is a forgotten case, unexplored within the red covers of the *Notable British Trials* series, or in the multitude of volumes that exist on unsolved murders. Madeleine Smith, Oscar Slater, William Gardiner, Florence Maybrick - all are well-known to the student of crime. But Charles Angus remains a denizen of an age further back, elusive and unknown. Tall, stout, and curly haired, he stood his trial at the Lancaster Assizes for the murder of his children's governess, Margaret Burns. The jury came back with a verdict, but the court hadn't heard the truth.

Truth, it is said, lies at the bottom of a deep well.

In the Angus case, a stone dropped into that well seems to fall for ever.

❦ ❦ ❦

1 The Merchant

In the year 1785, a young man chose to leave his native Scotland, and travel south to make his fortune in the port of Liverpool. His name was Charles Angus, and he possessed that genius for thrift, shrewdness and hard work that would serve so many of his countrymen during the industrial age.

The fifth child of a barber, he was born in Stranraer, Wigtownshire, a small town on the west coast of Scotland that relied largely on the coasting and fishing trade. With Belfast just forty miles away across the sea, the streets of the tiny port swarmed with Irish hawkers who came to barter their native linen for old woollen clothes with which they returned laden to their own shores. That these 'troglers' preferred the warm clothing of Scotland even to gold and silver was a source of great curiosity and amusement to the locals. But a traveller from the landward side would see a very different aspect. To the east was the wild and desolate Galloway hill country, a tract of land across which it took a brave man to venture, the home of bandits and black cattle. Few English travelled to this part of the country, or beyond. 'North Britain', the name given to everything on the Scottish side of the border, was another country, another land, dangerous and uncivilised, where distances were vast, roads impossible, and the inhabitants a strange species of mortal.

The pole jutting forth from over William Angus' barber shop door, with its stripes of red and blue to symbolise the arterial and venous blood, and symbolic brass basin to represent the utensil for the letting of blood, were all that remained of the old surgical pretensions of the barber-surgeons. Nevertheless, William Angus' services were in great demand. The craft of 'barbourising', to use the expression of the day, was one of the largest and most prosperous in the community. Gentlemen were dependent on their barbers to make their wigs and shave their heads, particularly on the Sabbath, when doubtless William Angus furtively bore his customers' wigs all over Stranraer, ready trimmed for worship, running the gauntlet of the Kirk treasurer whose job it was to levy fines on Sabbath breakers. The church came down as hard on the barbers as it did on the whisky retailers. In between, William Angus found time to father twelve children, a 'barber's dozen' so to speak. His wife, Janet McDowall (women did not change their names on marriage in Scotland), was most probably a descendant of the McDowalls on the Mull of Galloway, that emerald green peninsula of farming land that points south across the Irish Sea towards the Isle of Man.

Charles Angus first saw the pale, watery light of a lowland day on the 4th of September, 1767. It is tempting to romanticise and say that the choice of name betrays a sympathy for the Jacobite cause, whose most famous adherent, the Bonnie Prince, had swept through Scotland twenty-odd years before in an attempt to regain the throne. Of his brothers and sisters born later, three would feature prominently in his life, William and Alexander, born in 1771 and 1775 respectively, and Elizabeth, born in 1780, the youngest and the last of the offspring.

Charles was eighteen when he decided to leave Stranraer and make the perilous journey to England. He was a tall youth, in search of adventure, living in a small backwater whose sons were bred for the sea, or a living associated with it. Whether he travelled south on a sailing packet, or did what many of his countrymen did - rode a horse and sold it at his destination - it was the start of what he would later call his 'journey through life'.

The sights that met his eyes in the Liverpool of his day must have taken his breath away. Sedan chairs swung through narrow streets, bearing rich merchants from their Georgian mansions to their counting houses near the docks. It was the summer of that year when the celebrated aeronaut Lunardi visited the town with his hot air balloon and ascended to great applause from the fort, coming down safely in Simon's Wood. Handel's *Messiah* boomed out from St Peter's Church, a celebration of music and culture. The London mail coach would rattle in after a thirty-hour journey, horn rasping, guard and coachman armed with blunderbusses, to a population eager to hear the news from the capital. Peace had been restored after the end of the American War of Independence, and after what had seemed like a century of conflicts with France, it was almost palpable. It could be felt, breathed, smelt. It wouldn't last, but while it did, Liverpool was going to make the most of it.

The real life-blood of the port was down by the docks. Merchant ships being loaded with ironware from the forges of the black country and with fabrics from the Lancashire mills; tradesmen plying everything from ships' screws to black ginger, hogsheads to carpets, timber to elephants' teeth; while press-gangs roamed the waterfront at night, drifting in and out of low taverns, roping in the unwary for, if not a life, at least a year on the ocean wave. It was the age of Jolly Jack Tar, pigtailed British seamen, and the waterfront harlots who spread more than momentary happiness around the pier head. Just off shore, the masts and sails of tea-clippers, Atlantic brigs and Greenland whalers made a splendid sight. 'The mercantile world,' said the Liverpool papers, 'is in a hurry and bustle unknown at any former time. The merchants are endeavouring to outstrip each other in the race of traffic'. Liverpool was at the helm, with the most extensive docks in England. But there was another element to all this industry, all this frenetic mercantile activity, all this shipping.

That element was slavery.

Charles Angus could not have been unaware of it as he took lodgings and searched for a job. It was said at the time that two thirds of the population were directly or indirectly involved in the slave trade. For a young man interested in shipping, commerce or slavery, Liverpool was a boom town, bursting with opportunity. Newspaper advertisements invited men of adventurous spirit to 'try their luck'. The slave trade was a triangular business - seagoing merchants set forth from the bustling port, the holds of their ships laden with merchandise with which to barter for slaves on the African coast. There, the holds would be refilled with their miserable human cargo, and the ship would set sail again, on what was known as the middle passage, to America and the West Indian colonies. The demand for slaves in the colonies was insatiable - and thus the second point of the triangle was drawn. The slaves, many dying after the long passage, were put ashore and sold, the slave decks speedily reconstructed, and the holds filled with commodities from the plantations of the New World to which the British had become addicted - tobacco and sugar. With the unloading of these new necessities back in Liverpool, tobacco for the pipes of the Englishmen, and sugar to sweeten the puddings with which his tea table groaned, the triangle was closed. Within its three sides, much abject human misery existed. But at the end of the eighteenth century, it was the rock upon which Liverpool would become fat and prosperous.

Charles Angus' first job, and one he would hold for many years, was in a druggist's counting house. The dispensing druggist was a new breed of medical entrepreneur. They were seen as totally untrained, ignorant opportunists, mere grocers who had invaded the territory long held by the apothecaries. Angus became fascinated by medicine. Perhaps it was the redundant surgical pretensions of his father's occupation that provided the spark. He studied Bell on the venereal disease, and no doubt possessed a copy of Buchan's *Domestic Medicine*, a standard work which advocated warm asses' milk for cases of consumption, sea-water for piles, and extract of Peruvian bark for practically everything from epilepsy to gout. It was the era of folk remedies, when physicians were generally distrusted, and apothecaries and druggists dispensed such wonderful sounding remedies as Virginian snake root and salts of hartshorn.

Little is known of Angus' first ten years in the port. As a mere druggist's assistant, he did not feature in the Liverpool directory as a principal inhabitant, and would not reach that exalted position until the turn of the century. It is clear, however, that he applied himself studiously, graduated from merely copying out the names of medicines to dispensing them himself, and treating patients. He also, by his own admission, began instructing young persons to be doctors and getting them situations aboard African ships.

That is probably putting too fine a gloss on it. The young men whom he 'instructed' were largely quacks and drunken incompetents who were down on their luck, and who saw a voyage aboard a slave ship as a means of making money or escaping debt or paternity. It was a miserable occupation. Surgeons aboard slaveships were powerless to stop the spread of contagious and horrible diseases like smallpox. More common, however, was dysentery, or the bloody flux, which left the tightly squeezed and chained slaves in a quagmire of their own excrement, all the worse in stormy weather when they could not be taken up on deck and exercised. As it was a belief in those days that merely the smell could cause the disease, it was the surgeon's task to keep the slave decks clean, and many, for obvious reasons, never bothered. There is no evidence that Angus ever sailed on one of those hell-holes to the New World, but he could not have been unaware of the conditions in which his trainees would have to work. One can only hope that the primitive education he offered was equal to the task.

As ten years of peace drew to an end, and the century neared its violent and bloody close with Napoleon's might growing every month across the channel, a sea-change occurred in Angus' fortunes. Daily he must have watched the prosperous merchants strutting down from their mansion houses in their breeches and waistcoats and double-breasted jackets, the more old-fashioned of them still with powdered hair, to their places of business. Few had more education than befitted a counting house, but they contributed not only to their own pockets but to the social and commercial well-being of the town. Many owned their own ships. Even leading shopkeepers would join now and then in the venture to foreign lands. Others would set up ad-hoc companies and buy shares in some overseas expedition, and after sharing the profits, liquidate the company. A testament to the mark made by these men on the town is the fact that at least twenty-six Liverpool streets are named after then.

Angus soon joined their ranks. He was never destined to be a leading merchant, with a street sign bearing his name or a charitable institution boasting him as a founder member, but in branching out as a general merchant he seems to have been moderately successful and happy. He soon had his own counting house, and was following in the tradition of many Galloway sons, developing a 'Scotch commercial business' and expanding to deal with manufacturers in Ireland and the Isle of Man. He formed a partnership with a fellow countryman, Robert Copland, and together they traded out of premises in Mersey Street, but after a few years this partnership was dissolved. Billinge's *Advertiser* for October 14th 1799 informs us that,

CHARLES ANGUS HAS ON SALE
A few pieces of fine pale Holland Geneva of great strength
(Holland Geneva was gin)
Real Cognac Brandy of Superior Strength and flavour
Scotch carpeting, elegant patterns at reduced prices
Pickled Salmon suitable for the Italian market
Quebec Pipe, American Hogshead and Barrel Staves
Ships' screws, Capsterns, and Spindles

By the end of November, Angus had sold everything but a 'few pieces of Holland Geneva of full import strength, pale colour and excellent flavour' plus 'real Cognac Brandy' which is now of a quality 'not to be equalled in the market'. His salesmanship appears to have worked, for he does not advertise again until early in the first year of the new century, when along with Holland Geneva of great strength we find him selling,

New - Pickled Salmon, of this year's catch, of high perfection, fit for home use, and admirable coloured for a foreign maker. MESS PORK.

The pickled salmon may have found its way onto gentlemen's tables, but the mess pork was for the crews manning the slave ships and other merchant vessels, some now equipped for war and engaged at the mouth of the River Mersey as floating batteries, in readiness against French invasion. Angus also offered for sale around this time a twelve hundredweight ship's anchor, plus 'half barrels of newly cured red herrings', an item not without its irony in the light of future events.

Although he had given up being a druggist's assistant he never lost his interest in medicine. This led him one day to boast about a taboo subject in which he had educated his 'young doctors'. The counting house below his own was occupied by a timber merchant, Peter

Charnley, who was only a year or so from retiring. Angus and Charnley had become in Charnley's words 'intimate', and would spend many of their leisure hours together. On one of these occasions their conversation turned to the subject of unwanted pregnancies. Angus claimed he knew how to terminate such a condition, and produced an instrument specially designed for the purpose. It was a long silver tube through which ran a slide with a sharp three-edged dart at the tip. Charnley took it in his hands, and pushed the slide up and down, observing that to use such a thing to deliberately cause a miscarriage was a great sin. Angus supposedly answered, 'The sin is in taking away life, not in preventing it', though he would later vehemently deny that he had ever countenanced abortion. It was an exchange he would live to regret.

Whether or not Angus really believed that taking away life was a sin - and the slave trade took away millions of lives - he was soon to join that enterprising band of merchants who dealt in human cargoes. It stemmed from his marriage to a young girl with the romantic sounding name of Maria McQuistin.

2 Marriage into Money

When Angus first met Maria McQuistin, he was a young man in his twenties and she was probably in her puberty. She was the daughter of Thomas McQuistin, a wealthy coffee plantation owner and livestock breeder from Jamaica, who with his wife Jane decided to retire to Liverpool around the year 1796. In the Liverpool *Directory* for that year, he describes his profession as a 'gent'. Given the appalling reputation of Jamaican slave owners of that period, it is likely that to modern eyes he was as much a true gentleman as Angus was a physician.

Thomas McQuistin owned a house in Spanish Town called Turnberry, plus six hundred acres of land in the north of the country under the shadow of Mount Diablo called St. Faith's Penn, with horses, mules, horned cattle and eighty slaves. Jamaica had been a British colony for well over a century, but it was still a frontier, in which plantation owners and their families lived often isolated lives. In the year the McQuistins moved to Liverpool, Jamaica had erupted into slave revolt. The trouble had been brewing for decades. Local Maroons and rebellious runaway slaves had formed fiercely independent communities resistant to control, and were beginning to take on British forces with alarming results. Plantation owners and their families were being attacked in their settlements. It was no longer safe to travel. The island was flooded with rumours about French conspiracies to unleash the slave labour in a wave of rebellion. It was in this atmosphere of fear and paranoia that the McQuistins decided to pack up and come to Liverpool, leaving their property and 'negro stock' in the hands of overseers. Thomas McQuistin was getting on in years, and in common with most slave owners, had no desire to spend the autumn of his life in a land which had never seemed like home.

Thomas McQuistin was of Irish descent. It may be unfair to brand him with the same iron that is used by historians to brand all slave owners, but his activities were colourful to say the least. He already had four illegitimate children when, in 1771, he married a mulatto, or half negro, called Sarah Richards. White slave owners frequently bedded their domestic black slaves, and the offspring of these unions had become a class apart from both whites and blacks. Coloured women often saw marriage to a slave owner as a way of improving their lot, and in marrying Thomas McQuistin, Sarah Richards had secured for any children a better life. In this she was right. Though one of her children died of fever at the age of four, the other, Thomas, received a favour in his father's will many years later when Thomas McQuistin bequeathed 'two hundred pounds of current money of Jamaica to free Thomas McQuistin, quadroon man'. An even more telling instruction in the will is the bequest of five hundred pounds to 'all and every the legitimate and illegitimate children or child of Adam Rose McQuistin', suggesting that Adam Rose, yet another illegitimate child, was a chip off the old block. He and his sister Mary Rose were the offspring of an already free quadroon, or quarter negro, called Lucretia Rose. The baptism and burial register for the parish of St Catherine's in Jamaica is littered with quarter and half-coloured McQuistins of dubious legitimacy.

One entry reads simply:

RICHARD A mulato McQuistin Christened June 6th 1772

For baby Richard to have been a mulatto, his mother had to be black. The old planter had plenty of seed in him.

When Sarah died, Thomas turned to a recently widowed white woman, Jane Burns, whose first husband had also been a slave owner. White women were snapped up with indecent haste in the colonies since they were in such short supply. He was then sixty -eight, she was only twenty-four with two children of her own, Margaret and John Burns. The fruit of their union was Maria, born on March 21st, 1786. She was Thomas McQuistin's only white child, and would have heaped upon her all the love and privileges of her birthright.

She was brought up, pampered by black servants, and like all white children growing up in that steamy hothouse environment adopted much of the black slaves' speech and many of their mannerisms. White children were almost reared by black servants on the slave islands. Maria's short life must have been deeply influenced by the slave songs and stories and culture of the black domestics in the plantation home. As for her mother Jane, it need only be said that the plantation homes were no place for white women while their husbands drank and brutalised the slaves. They searched for their own pleasures in town, while no doubt dreaming of English shores and thinking how much more safe and civilised life could be.

When Maria was old enough she was despatched to England to receive a 'complete female education' at a boarding school, and this may well account for Angus' introduction to her. Merchants at home frequently acted as guardians to the children of West Indian traders who were sent across the sea to be educated. Many years later Angus would perform such a role for another Jamaican planter, writing of 'the charge you honour me with in trusting to my love your only daughter . . . from the moment your child falls under my direction, your anxiety may cease. I will act towards her as if she were my own'.

Maria received a female education that Angus in later years would consider too complete. English, writing, accounts, geography and plain sewing were in his opinion the most useful subjects, with dancing and Latin to be attended to later. He did not approve of ornamental sewing, nor was he an advocate of the nightly habit young ladies had in such institutions of exchanging ideas on 'improper subjects'.

Thomas and Jane McQuistin arrived in Liverpool after weeks on a pitching, rolling sea, more than likely coming ashore with airs, graces and dialects that might bewilder someone who had never left British shores. Of Jane's two children by her former marriage, John Burns appears to have come home for a time and then returned to Jamaica, while Margaret Burns, after living with the family for a while, would go to London and work as a governess. Of Margaret Burns, we shall have much to learn later.

It would not do to live anywhere near the waterfront - that was the mercantile quarter with its inns and low life, and besides, the river Mersey often rose and flooded the lower ends of Chapel and Water Street (the latter being well named). The poor, mainly Irish emigrants, lived by the river, in squalid rat-infested houses that were frequently washed by storms. Not only that, but many of the older streets were narrow, crooked, and disagreeable to walk down. The footpaths, or parapets, were clammy and dirty and laid with sharp pebbles, and there was always the risk of tumbling to oblivion down a projecting cellar. Heaps of dirt, two feet deep, raked up by the scavengers, lay for days in hot weather, stinking and offensive, and at night were a positive danger to lung and limb. They had earned the name of 'corporation beds' from a tradition that local worthies, returning from evenings of hospitality at the Town Hall, might be found drunk and asleep in them.

The house in which Thomas McQuistin chose to hang up his planter's hat was in the newer, more respectable district around St Anne Street, almost as far from the river as one could get. Number Two, Trinity Place, was a dignified and 'commodious' three-storey townhouse with a large garden, tucked in behind Trinity Church, in a narrow thoroughfare that connected Springfield Street and King Street (later to be Wilton Street). The location was high and dry, the neighbours were of the professional class - merchants, insurance brokers, doctors, clergymen - and the other houses either side of the church were equally pleasant places of residence. In summer, it must have been an enchanting place to live, with the hum of bees in Trinity Churchyard, and the rolling hills of Everton with their farmhouses and snug white cottages to the north, and open countryside to the east. What a far cry from the hazardous life of the tropics, with its diseases and chain gangs of slaves and ever-present threat of rebellion. For Maria, who had now completed her female education, it was a return to a family home, where her learning would ultimately be put to good use as a wife and mother.

Angus was to do very well out of his association with the McQuistins. Thomas McQuistin, who was in his eighties and in failing health, consented to the marriage between Angus and his daughter, and made it clear he wished his prospective son-in-law to conduct all his affairs for him, both at home and abroad. Having dissolved his mercantile partnership with Robert Copland, Angus was now the active member in a slave trading partnership called Angus, Dale and Co. This almost certainly meant he had put up the largest investment while the others were merely sleeping partners whose involvement was limited to investing a smaller share and receiving a corresponding share of the profits. In all probability Thomas McQuistin had given Angus the necessary financial help.

Angus was soon employing three young men in his counting house, while owning two slaveships, the Huntingdon, under a Captain Phillips, with three hundred and forty-one slaves on board, and the Minerva, under Captain Much, with three hundred and seventy negroes, both bound for Kingston, Jamaica. In his letter book, which he kept fastidiously, he recorded in a letter to Adam Rose McQuistin at Spanish Town, one of the old man's illegitimate offspring,

'Mr McQuistin has expressed a desire to have some okra and some fruit home, he will take it kind if you send him some okra, yams, shaddocks, grapefruit, all packed carefully in a cask, and shipped on board one of my own ships, then it will come freight free.'

He also requested that 'some elegant conch shells of elegant colours' be sent home for young Maria to use as chimney-piece ornaments.

On the 5th March, 1800, Thomas McQuistin gave his official consent (as was required by law) before George Monk, curate, to the marriage between 'Charles Angus of the Parish of Liverpool, Merchant' and his daughter Maria 'aged 15 years and a minor'. Actually, she was two weeks away from her fourteenth birthday. In an age when girls could be married as young as twelve, it was still unusual enough an event to elevate the odd eyebrow. Angus' signature on the wedding bond is a bold, flourishing piece of calligraphy, while Thomas McQuistin's betrays an older, shakier and more faltering hand.

It is easy to say that Angus was marrying into money, even easier to say that at thirty-three he was old enough to be Maria's father. What gives one pause for thought is that when he was first contemplating marriage to her she was probably small enough and young enough to bounce on his knee.

They were married three days later at St Nicholas' Church, the parochial and oldest church of Liverpool, and a landmark for returning mariners. Perched right on the quayside and weathered by tremendous storms, it had long been known as the 'sailor's church' before which departing seamen had been accustomed to leave offerings as a protection against piracy, shipwreck and other hazards of the high seas. As Angus stepped out of the church into the fresh sea breeze, with his child bride on his arm, he might well have been advised to leave an offering himself. As he looked up and immediately south, to the bottom end of Water Street, he could not have missed a grim castellated structure, its gloomy forbidding walls giving it the appearance of a fort. This was the Borough Gaol, or 'Tower', Liverpool's notorious prison.

He was not to know on such a happy day that it lay across the path of his journey through life.

3 Storm Clouds

Richard Statham was furious. A solicitor by profession, and the assistant to the Town Clerk of Liverpool, he had in front of him a note from a wealthy client requesting that all his papers be sent home, and informing him that he no longer wished Statham to act as his solicitor. The matter which had prompted this insult was the drawing up of a new will to which, outrage upon outrage, he was no longer invited to be executor. The will was that of Thomas McQuistin, and the person behind Statham's removal as solicitor and executor was Charles Angus, who was now living with his wife at Trinity Place.

A contemporary sketch of Richard Statham shows him to have been a Pickwickian-looking character with puffy jowls, beetling eye-brows, and duckfeathers of hair wisping out from the back of a bald head. A true Liverpool worthy, he had sat on the committee which conducted the festivities of April 1788, when a grand ball and banquet were held to celebrate the restoration of King George III to health after a period of madness. He had with public spirit given fifty pounds to the government two years before for the defence of the country (many Liverpool worthies gave more). His father had been an attorney in Liverpool before him, and his uncle the town postmaster, whom many remembered operating from a little hole in his window in a simple dwelling in John Street. One prominent physical attribute of Richard Statham was the size of his pos-terior. A leading Tory supporter, he would be later satirised in an election pamphlet as one of the participants in an ass race, riding a beast called Allbum.

Not a man to be crossed, or to act in haste, Richard Statham bided his time. The will which Angus' father-in-law intended drawing up, only three months after the marriage, favoured Angus enormously, and Angus must have felt that Statham would be greatly opposed to it. We only have Angus' word for what transpired, from his evidence at the trial. A day or two later 'not deigning to wait on the old gentleman the evening the note was delivered, and choosing to suit his own time in calling', Richard Statham turned up at Trinity Place and began behaving in a very 'boisterous and unprofessional manner'. According to Angus, he seemed to forget that he was out of his department in the Liverpool Exchange, where presumably he had the authority to rant and rage. Thomas McQuistin, we learn, 'passed the insult over in peace, age having cooled the ardour of the old gentleman's mind'. Had he possessed his youthful vigour, Angus informs us, 'Mr Statham would have cringed where he now stormed'.

Doubtless the old planter's youthful vigour had served him well back in Jamaica. Now it was Angus' youthful vigour that seemed to be the dominant force. Richard Statham left Trinity Place without the satisfaction of bending his client's will, convinced even more that Angus was in no small measure behind it. Almost certainly he viewed Angus as an opportunist while Angus regarded Statham as someone who, as executor, could be deliberately obstructive. It wasn't the last Angus had heard of the portly solicitor, however. Liverpool was too small a town for that. The seeds of revenge were sown, and would germinate.

As executors, Thomas McQuistin called on a Liverpool merchant, Thomas Fletcher, and his friend and family physician, Henry Park. Fifty-five years old, and descended from an ancient Liverpool family, Park would become known for a pioneering act of conservative surgery, when he removed the diseased knee-joint of a sailor in an age when sawing off the leg would have been more standard procedure. The sailor lived on to be twice shipwrecked without further complaint. Probably those two gentleman combined were more malleable than the obdurate Richard Statham.

In his will, Thomas McQuistin left the house to his wife Jane, who also benefited from a settlement made before their marriage, plus fifty and a hundred pounds respectively to the two children by her former marriage, Margaret and John Burns. After disposing of various sums to his children and grandchildren in Jamaica, he then turned to the bulk of his estate which incorporated all the 'plantations, penns, woodlands, buildings, store houses and stock negroes' plus a sum of sixteen thousand pounds owed to him by another planter. This he left in its entirety to his 'dearly beloved daughter Maria' should she reach the age of twenty-one or have 'issue of her body'. Until such time, the estate was to be held and managed by the executors, who were to pay Maria the annual income from it. She was going to be a very rich young lady. But what was so startling was the provision that even if Maria died before she reached twenty-one, and without having children, most of the estate was still to be settled on his son-in-law. Angus' star was firmly in the ascendant.

Invested now with full power to conduct all his father-in-law's affairs, Angus was doing just that, sending out letters to an attorney in Jamaica demanding an inventory and circumstantial details of the state of St Faith's Penn, requesting an account of all male and female slaves, horses, mules and horned cattle, and offering to send out any articles needed for the upkeep of the Penn at a cheaper rate. Angus was nothing if not an opportunist. Paternalistic by nature, overbearing and pompous, his character is best illuminated by a letter he sent to his wife's half brother, John Burns, only a week after his marriage. John Burns was engaged as a book-keeper, back in Jamaica, on an estate called Roaring River.

'My dear Fellow, I must certainly take the liberty to rally you on the score of your bad writing. Surely it will not disgrace you to take pains to write better, no excuse can atone for the unpardonable neglect of attention. You will know what patient pains I took to induce you to improve your hand of write, you seem not to attend to it. As long as I see you attentive and displaying a wish to act up to the repeated advices I have given you, you will find me an indulgent good brother, but if you disregard my injunctions and in contradiction to my will trample upon all my advices and blast them with innattentiveness and carelessness, you know me so well as to give you little hope of expecting good from me. Suppose, my Dear Boy, I had been as careless and thoughtless as you seem to set out, would I have sat in the situation I do today? No John! I might yet have been the servant of servants.'

It is hardly surprising to learn that John Burns never bothered to reply. Maria's half brother kept his silence for many years, in spite of letters from Angus demanding news of him.

Thomas McQuistin set his hand to his will on the 20th June, 1800. Four weeks later he was dead. He was eighty-two years old, and the age was not conducive to longevity. His years in the tropics had doubtless taken their toll. As he was carried across Trinity Place, through the wooden gates of Trinity Churchyard, and laid to rest in the family vault, there must have been those in Liverpool - Richard Statham among them - who harboured the suspicion that Angus had helped him on his way.

Maria wasted no time in giving Angus 'issue of her body'. Their first daughter, Jane, arrived the following year, and in August 1802 they had a second daughter, whom they christened Maria. She was not yet seventeen years old.

Angus was further favoured by an invitation to join the Athenaeum, membership of which was fast becoming a hallmark of social standing in the town. This grand institution, which still exists in Liverpool, was then a square classical building at the corner of Church Street. It was a library and news-room, where the professional classes of the town could indulge their taste for the higher brands of knowledge, safely closeted from the uncouth military men who swarmed around the port, taking over coffee houses, taverns, and the previously favoured Lyceum Club. Subscribers each bought a share in the club, which when relinquished would be passed on to someone else waiting to join. At first the list of subscribers was limited to 350, but the following year another seventy-five shares were created, and Angus became the 388th member, paying twenty guineas for the privilege. Once inside its hallowed portals, members could read the newspapers, which included *The Times* brought by post-chaise from London, use the members' coffee room, and utilise the library which after only three years in existence boasted over six thousand volumes, many in Greek, Latin and Oriental languages. Undoubtedly it was also a hotbed of masculine gossip. Common tradesmen were excluded. On the membership list were lawyers, doctors, bankers, merchants, clergymen and architects. Angus had come a long way from being a druggist's assistant. In the parish register at the christening of his second daughter, he does not describe his occupation as a merchant at all, but as a 'gentleman'. In Georgian England, to be a gentleman was to arrive.

Two other Anguses arrived in Liverpool at that time, giving the appearance of a gathering of the clan. Alexander Angus, another of the barber's dozen, and Charles' youngest brother, came down from Stranraer and set up in business as an insurance broker, living a few doors round the corner in King Street. A young man 'of the first respect and of the fairest prospects' he would make himself a fortune, though his life would end in tragedy. Insurance was developing rapidly in response to the needs of the slave trade. Not only vessels needed cover (and many sailed without) but the merchandise too. This became painfully apparent when the vast pile of the Goree warehouses at George's Dock, where the Liverpool merchants stored their goods, burnt down one terrible night, destroying £323,000 worth of property and causing the collapse of the company which had only just insured them. Clearly there were fortunes to be made - and lost.

The second Angus was Charles' twenty-year-old sister Elizabeth. She had been only five when he left Scotland. He must have been very fond of his sister. He acted as bondsman, and was a witness at her own wedding at St Peter's Church in Liverpool only a fortnight after his own, to another Galloway man, William Biggam. Biggam, who had been brought up a farmer, would subsequently set up in business in Brunswick Street as a cabinet maker. There was not one trade or department of business or profession in England where Scots were not making their careers with pertinacious success, and Liverpool was full of them.

Unfortunately an ill wind was beginning to blow the tide of Angus' fortunes. As a slave trader and merchant, Angus knew all about ill winds. When they were favourable, the Mersey was a marvellous sight, full of ships in sail departing from the quayside, while crowds gathered to cheer them on and wives bade long farewells to their loved ones. When they were not, there was nothing to do but wait. What happened to Angus was a salutary lesson that even in the boom time, a Liverpool slave trader could come unstuck. Part of the problem he summed up in a letter to an unscrupulous Jamaican merchant when he wrote of his intention to 'steer clear of designing West India merchants in future' and of 'how little one on this side of the water can do to prevent those taking advantage on your side'.

Angus' overseas adventure had gone disastrously wrong, losing him and Angus, Dale and Co, a great deal of money. To start with he had been unlucky enough to lose not only two of his ships and at least as many cargoes, but three of his captains as well. The Minerva, which had departed from the African coast with three hundred and seventy slaves, had arrived in Jamaica, where Captain Much had instructions to sell the vessel for no less than £2,500. Unfortunately the Captain never made it. The same unscrupulous Jamaican merchant had seized the ship, had a false survey carried out on her, had her condemned, and bought her himself for £500. In the summer of 1801, Angus fitted out a small brig called the Blanche for one hundred and eighty-six slaves, plus two cosily named vessels, the Plumper and the Friendship. The fate of the Friendship and its cargo was anything but cosy. She had three hundred slaves on board which Angus intended selling for seventy five pounds each, but on the death of its captain, the chief mate landed the ship in Barbados where it was seized, and the slaves sold for nearer half that amount. Angus did receive 'payment' for the slaves, but in the form of false packed sugar which he was forced to sell in Liverpool at a vast loss.

Angus' bad luck had elements of farce. He possessed some 'fine views of Wales and Ireland, chiefly landscapes, elegantly framed and glazed' which he wished to part with so that he could buy oil paintings instead. He gave them into the care of one of his captains with instructions to sell them in the West Indies (possibly to some homesick planter), but the captain was shot dead in a duel and the views disappeared somewhere on the island of Dominique.

There was however the potential income from St Faith's Penn in Jamaica, which Angus had been told should clear three thousand pounds a year. Even in this he was thwarted. Not so much as a penny from the property found its way to the emptying coffers at Trinity Place. The reasons for this are probably many, chief among them the fact that the land had been plundered by his late father-in-law's illegitimate children, nothing had been planted, and a number of the slaves had run off. The property was in the hands of an attorney called George Kinghorn, whose predecessor in Angus' words had been a great scoundrel. Informed that a female slave was missing, he wrote angrily:

'There is a female slave Patience, are her children in Kingston, get to know the reason of her being off the property, and make them be accounted for one way or another . . . when the negroes are on the property, first thing you cause them to do is repair all the walls, clear all the pasture ground, and when completely cleared . . . purchase lean stock of a good breed'.

Nothing appears to have been done. By February 1803 the property had still yielded nothing. Angus' frustration mounted. He could of course have stepped on a ship to Jamaica and gone over there to sort things out himself, as he was tempted to do, but Maria wouldn't let him. He wrote,

'I am trying every argument in my power to persuade Mrs Angus to allow me to go over and see to the state of affairs, although she seems repugnant to it. Think she will consent. It may seem curious to you that I am restrained by her, but, a matter of such consequence I would not choose to act upon without her concurrence'.

Curious indeed. The man who would berate his wife's half brother for the slackness of his handwriting was at least afraid of somebody. Angus' solution to the problem was to send out another of his brothers from Stranraer to manage the property, and for the task he selected thirty-two-year-old William. It is a grim irony that in an age when the spelling of names was wildly variable, William Angus should have been christened William Anguish. He would live up to the name. By August of that year, young William was on St Faith's Penn and taking charge or doing whatever it was that William deemed 'taking charge' meant.

After receiving a melancholy account of the Penn, Angus wrote to William requesting him to plant more provisions and grass, to job out as many of the negroes as he could (many of the negro men had trained as mechanics) and to sell off all the fatted stock he could spare and buy breeding cattle. Six months later he had heard nothing. He wrote:

'The whole management of the Penn is in your trust. Business is very uncertain . . . God forbid if the direction of the property might fall into the hands of such plunderers as those who preceded you, and leave us little better than beggars, which is what I dread . . . Times in this country are truly bad, little going on but soldiering, taxes very heavy . . . If you could once begin to send even a few hundred pounds a year, I would soon, with my present economical way of living, get the ball off my foot.'

If Angus thought that putting a member of his own family on the Penn meant that it would start to provide him with an income, he was sadly mistaken. As for Maria, whose property it was, her fear was that her father's other children would try to take possession of it. 'Mrs Angus does not consider her father's bastard children any relatives', Angus wrote.

There were periods of happiness. The family spent three summer months in 1803 back over the border in Galloway, where Angus shot a large number of sea birds. He was particularly proud of his gun, an elegant substantial steel-mounted weapon with a barrel nearly five feet long, which cost him eight guineas. He boasted that the barrel was longer than that of his brother Alexander's gun, and wrote to William in Jamaica that as they were all to be soldiers in Liverpool, he was keeping it to shoot Bonaparte with should he ever have the impudence to land there.

Yet another Angus made his appearance in June the following year when Maria gave birth to their third child, a boy whom they called Thomas McQuistin Angus. Henry Park attended the birth as family physician, in which capacity he had attended the births of both girls. In his register of deliveries he recorded for the third time that the birth was natural. Nevertheless the strain on Maria was probably great - she was still only eighteen - and there is evidence that her health was failing. Angus would later claim that he had had to sit up with her for six months. Not surprisingly, the poor girl was probably exhausted.

It was for this reason that it was decided to employ a governess to look after the children, and Maria's half-sister Margaret Burns was invited to come and live with the family to take up not only that position but that of housekeeper as well. Having a governess was then the height of fashion. During and after the Revolution, the French had been arriving in Britain in droves, bringing all sorts of new ideas with them that aspiring middle-class families were keen to emulate. Angus was no doubt aspiring to be as middle-class as the rest of his neighbours up and down the length of St Anne Street, not to mention his fellow members of the Athenaeum.

As she stepped through the doorway of Number Two, Trinity Place, Margaret Burns probably had little awareness of how fashionable a commodity she had become. Or that it was the last position she would ever take up.

4 A Martyr to the Dropsy

Governesses of the period were frequently females who were down on their luck and on the shelf. Margaret Burns was no exception.

Evidence is scanty as to what she had been doing since arriving with the family from Jamaica. Gore's *Liverpool Directory* for 1804, the year of her arrival at Trinity Place, records that she had been keeping a small shop in Clement's Street, just off the Vauxhall Road, though it fails to state what kind of shop. It must have been a short and unsuccessful venture as the entry only appears for that one year. Before that, she had been a governess in London, but had spent at least some of her time with the family in Liverpool, for in 1798 her mother, Jane McQuistin, had taken her to the Liverpool Infirmary to be strongly electrified by Dr Minshull for 'an obstruction in her female evacuations'.

Her state of health would become a matter of great controversy. She was a small, broad-chested woman with a pale and sallow complexion, and was a martyr to the dropsy. To her intimate friends she confided that she would be carried off by it, as 'broad-chested people almost always went off in dropsies'. It was fashionable, of course, for Georgian women to portray themselves as delicate and suffering creatures, but Margaret Burns appears to have enjoyed exploring her imminent demise at every occasion. She would later claim that it was only infusions of powdered Peruvian bark in wine given her by Angus that had prevented her from finally teetering over the edge.

She also appears to have had more than a streak of parsimony in her nature. The same intimate friends, a girl called Elizabeth Jones and her mother who lived nearby in Hunter Street, would describe her as being of a 'close penurious nature' and of a 'careful turn', quaint expressions that would equally come to apply to Angus as we shall see. In fact it may as well be said now than later that the two of them, Charles Angus and Margaret Burns, possessed that one attribute which, at the time, brought so much prejudice upon the Scots - economy with money. From the outset, they were made for each other.

Her arrival at Trinity Place was hardly an upturn in her fortunes. To start with, she must have been a source of disappointment if not disgrace to her mother, Jane McQuistin. She was in her twenties and unmarried. One need only turn the pages of Jane Austen to garner an idea of prevailing social attitudes. It was every mother's ambition to marry off her daughters as early as possible to husbands who would take on the responsibility for them. Now here was her elder daughter by her first marriage coming back to live at home as little more than a servant.

Neither had the position of governess any social advantages attached to it whatsoever. It was very much a 'life between stairs'. Governesses traditionally were hated by the servants, who saw them as spies, yet they never properly became members of the family. Of course, Margaret Burns started off with the advantage that she was a member of the family, but this seems to have made little difference to the domestic arrangements. From the moment she arrived, she was packed upstairs to a room in the servants' quarters on the top floor. She wasn't even to have the pleasure of sleeping in her own room, for her duties soon came to involve sleeping with the children in the nursery below, across the landing from Angus' and Maria's bedroom. It was not unusual for a governess to be expected to share a bed with her young charges, and must have been a crushing invasion of her privacy. With Jane only two and a half years old, Maria one and half, and Thomas still a baby, it would be remarkable if she got any sleep at all.

When Angus returned to Stranraer, on visits to his family, Margaret Burns had responsibility for the health of the children, and would let herself into the wardrobe in Angus' bedroom when the necessity arose to spoon castor oil down their little throats. Fortunately, there were more pleasant duties, for both governess and children. When they became old enough, she would take Jane, Maria and Thomas the half-mile walk to Everton every morning to fetch milk and cream for breakfast. It must have been a pleasant treat for the children. In those days, Everton was a pretty village across rolling countryside where many of the wealthier merchants had their grand mansions, and where they kept their carriages in which they rode into Liverpool each day to do business. Once a barren sandstone ridge, it now flourished with tiers of well-kept gardens full of blossom and cascading greenery. The walk there and back on summer mornings, with the children playing in the long grass, and the scent of hay and honeysuckle in the air, must have been one of the few idyllic moments in her day.

Whether Margaret Burns harboured any jealousy towards her half-sister is difficult to know, but it would be expecting a great deal of human nature to imagine that she did not. She had inherited only fifty pounds under the terms of her stepfather's will a few years before, which was a smack in the face compared to the 'fortune' heaped upon Maria, even if that fortune was slow in materialising. It is possible she had a little money of her own, left to her by her natural father. A year into her employment Angus wrote that she had paid a visit to Edinburgh to 'perfect herself in a business' but she was soon back at Trinity Place, looking after her half-sister's children and catering to the domestic needs of her husband.

It must have rubbed salt in the wound, then, when her mother, not content with the proceeds of her second marriage, decided to embark on her third, this time to the Yeoman of the Silver Scullery of St James Palace in London. Jane McQuistin seems to have had an eye for a profitable or influential marriage. Her surviving letters reveal a woman much taken with the need to marry into social respectability. If marriage to two slave owners was hardly an opening into the best society, her third marriage at least took her into apartments at the Palace, where her new husband, Edward Williams, had the safekeeping of the Royal Plate and a staff of fifteen men under him just to keep it clean and safe. Angus spent three weeks at the Palace, on a wedding visit. His relationship with his mother-in-law had always been tricky. She was undoubtedly a match for him. When Angus had written to her son John Burns, on Roaring River Estate, Jamaica, telling him to return to Liverpool where he had procured a situation for him in a merchant's counting house, Jane McQuistin had written to her son telling him to stay exactly where he was.

Effectively, Jane McQuistin (or Jane Williams as she now was) disappears from the story for many years. The full implications of that disappearance will become of some importance.

Angus was now the master of Number Two, Trinity Place, and in his own way was eager to cultivate the best of connections. Yet under the mantle of gentleman, the young druggist's assistant was still peeking out and wanting to be heard. Angus had never lost his fascination for medicine. To his credit, in an age when child mortality was high, he must have doctored his own children well as not one of them succumbed in infancy.

A neighbour at that time was the Reverend James Gildart, a young man of twenty-six, and the curate of St Nicholas' Church where he had married Maria. One day they fell into conversation, probably about the things that were on everyones' lips - the ever-present threat from France and the impending mobilisation of the whole male population of the town from sixteen to sixty - when the conversation turned to something more down-to-earth. The subject arose (who raised it is not clear) respecting the marital state of a particular young lady who had found herself - to use the reverend gentleman's words - in a concealed marriage. Gildart expressed his opinion that such marriages were not safe 'for in a short time they might produce fruits'. This was grist to the mill for Angus.

According to Gildart, who like so many other people would remember such conversations, Angus said that he had studied medicine and could assure his friend that such effects might be prevented. This would seem to be rather an injudicious subject to bring up with a man of the cloth, even if the clergy in those days were a rather ribald fraternity. Angus once again would deny that he had ever sanctioned the use of abortion.

Haunting him now were his efforts to try to squeeze blood out of the stone that was St Faith's Penn. There had been a severe drought in Jamaica and many deaths, and Angus was concerned that he hadn't heard from William. He had been on the Penn for over a year and still no money was coming home to Liverpool. Worse, he had heard from his attorney in Kingston that the house in Spanish Town, which was also part of the estate, was now occupied by some of his father-in-law's 'bastard children'. To use the modern phrase, he had squatters.

Another demon was looming on the horizon, namely the abolition of the slave trade. The previous year, the motion had been made in the House of Commons, and carried by a majority of seventy-five. Little more remained to be done than to fix the period when the trade would cease absolutely. Angus, ever the opportunist, was determined to turn it to his advantage, and wrote to his Kingston attorney that it could not fail to have considerable effect in increasing the value of the slaves already on the property, as well as the value of the land. He may have been enriched by the thought. He wasn't enriched any other way. Sailing packet after sailing packet arrived in Liverpool from Jamaica, with no news from William and no promise of money.

Margaret Burns had been living in the house for less than eighteen months when tragedy again struck the family. Billinge's *Advertiser* for the 28th June 1805 carried a simple announcement in its death column. 'On Tuesday last, at her house, Trinity Place, Mrs Angus, wife of Charles Angus, Merchant'.

Maria had died of tuberculosis, from which she had suffered for nearly a year. Angus wrote to his brother, ever mindful of the need to mix bad news with business, as the next packet might be a long time sailing:

'Dear William, It is with foul rending grief I acquaint you of my much loved and ever to be lamented Maria's death . . . of a consumption. This event causes the Penn, Slaves and other Stock, with all landed property, thus immediately to fall under my own managements, however it is of little consequence seeing you persist in keeping silence and withholding accounts. I have now a young family left to my entire care, deprived of the tuition of one of the most amiable women and tender mothers. The task falls to my lot, May God, in his infinite goodness, assist and strengthen me, to acquit myself of the charge as a Good Man and father ought.'

To his nephew Robert Hornell in Antigua, he put it rather more emotively.

'I beg to inform you of the loss of my ever to be lamented Maria, who ceased to exist on Tuesday half past noon on 25th Ult, of a Pulmonary Consumption. Oh Sir, had you known her worth, you would have lamented her early death, few such amiable affectionate domestic women now exist.'

On the following Sunday, Maria was interred with her father in the family vault in Trinity Churchyard. Standing in the churchyard, clad in black, with Miss Burns and the three children by his side, Angus must have felt his enemies massing. He had married into property, his father-in-law had died only a month after making out his will, and now his child bride of just five summers ago was a corpse, two years away from her twenty-first birthday. In that short period she had given him 'issue of her body' three times over. Under the terms of Thomas McQuistin's will, the whole of the estate comprising the money held in trust, the 'plantations, penns, woodlands, buildings, store houses and stock negroes' would come to him and the children - if the executors and the courts did not drag their feet.

Jane and Maria would scarcely remember their young mother, and Thomas would not remember her at all. As the family turned from the grave, and walked out of the churchyard and across the road to the house, three motherless children had good reason to be thankful that their father had Miss Burns to take her place.

❦ ❦ ❦

5 Trouble on the Penn

A week after Maria's death, Angus heard from his brother William for the first time in a year. Six months later there was still no money forthcoming from St Faith's Penn. Christmas 1805 saw an angry letter dispatched by sailing packet from Liverpool to Jamaica. Angus pointed out that his brother-in-law, Mr Biggam, who had been brought up a farmer, had told him that in three years and with very little to begin on, they had completely stocked his father's farm, and with no-one to help the work forward but their own family. Why couldn't William turn the Penn round, with so many slaves to help him? Pleased however that William had a 'grand plan' which involved planting coffee, he tempered his anger with sound advice.

'It seems very odd you should be on a place of such extent for so many years, and yet no prospect of keeping itself. This, to all the agriculturalists consulted here, appears inexplicable. Am glad you are putting in more grass, it must pay one day, but coffee is your grand plan, plant it on every inch where the soil will yield it growth. Long on this, you will hear of the Armada being chased from the West Indies, and almost totally destroyed off Cape Trafalgar near Cadiz, by the ere to be lamented Nelson, who fell in action'.

The success of William's grand plan, however, remained elusive. Perhaps it too, like the gallant Nelson, had fallen in action. Two months later Angus got a letter back, in which William demanded a great sum in payment for his efforts.

'If you have been planting the coffee you say, and so much more I have recommended, is there no prospect of its pay? Coffee estates to others pay better than almost any! . . . Shall expect a very explicit answer to this letter, as it would be very unfortunate for me indeed to have the property fall under the guidance of the slaves'.

By the summer of 1806, the shadow of penury was growing longer, or at least Angus was eager to convey that impression. He had lost so much by his slave-trading adventure that the income from the Penn was all he had to look forward to. Angus Dale and Co, was now in the process of liquidation, one of the partners being in a precarious state of health, and the others going off into separate businesses. Angus and Copland of Mersey Street, back in the halcyon days when Angus had advertised his pickled salmon and Scotch carpets for sale, had long been dissolved, and his one time partner, Robert Copland was himself on the slippery road to bankruptcy.

By each packet Angus eagerly awaited news that the Penn was making a profit. By each packet, he was disappointed. His anger turned to self pity.

'I cannot divine what can occupy your time so very much, that you have never devoted any part of it to finishing [sic] and transmitting me accounts of all you have been doing. Taxes are exorbitant, my children growing, and all kinds of education very expensive. Even a hundred a year would help, which is a trifle to what you allow the Property can make, if stocked'.

According to Angus, he and his family were being forced to live on the meagre sum of five hundred pounds a year. His brother Alexander round the corner was doing much better, a fact which clearly galled him, for he wrote to William in September complaining,

'I, who am the oldest of the family, seem destined for the most pinching gripe of fortune. My brother has hitherto sailed down the smooth sea of Prosperity, you are in such situation that you live without giving account. William Biggam and my sister are doing as well as any can do in their line of business which is a good one, while I am obliged to live on a circumscribed income, and bring up a family genteely, at a time I had a right to expect much help from the Penn'.

He added, with some vitriol,

'From this date, cease to write me on politics. Let those whose business it is mind it!'

One can scarcely fail to picture Angus' reaction then when William's next letter informed him that even more of the slaves had run off. Not only that, but the house in Spanish Town, Turnberry, was still occupied and there was little hope of removing the occupants. Angus fired back an angry letter.

'It is singular I have been writing as long about the house in Spanish Town and never could get any information regarding it till now. Suppose it so bedevilled among them that I may conclude it lost to me . . . Could these runaway slaves never be got again? How is it you never advised me of even our runaways till now?! And now you do not say who they were!'

Angus' mother-in-law, safely ensconced in her ivory tower at St James Place, refused to believe that the property was not furnishing him with a handsome income. Angus wrote to her in some frustration assuring her that so far he had not had one penny from the estate, but to no avail. She had lived on the property, she knew its worth, she knew what it was capable of sending home. What she didn't know about, or what she perhaps closed her mind to, was the character of Angus' brother.

Inconsistencies now began creeping into William's letters, which confirmed Angus' suspicions that William was lying to him and not keeping copies of the letters he sent. Still Angus refused to accuse him of downright dishonesty, doubtless out of filial pride and doubtless because the devil he knew was a safer option than the devil he didn't. He had good justification. Angus learnt to his horror that he was paying colonial taxes for slaves which had been for years on the property of one of his father-in-law's bastard children.

The political ill wind for the merchants of Liverpool was now at
gale force. When William at last sent an inventory of the slaves, which
numbered eighty-nine including fourteen who were sick, seven runaways
and twenty-five children, Angus replied passionately,

'I set down at such a period to address you, and on such a time as
this country never saw. The abolition of the Slave Trade! Lord Graw has
got the Bill read a second time, engrossed, the Blanks filled up to be read
a third time in a few days, that no ship or vessel shall clear out from the
UK or their dependencies, on the Slave Trade after the first day of May
next (1807) and that no slaves shall be imported or sold in our colonies
after the first day of Jan 1808, that is allowing them barely time to conclude the voyages they may be upon. This will ehance the value of slaves
now on property, more than double.'

His instructions on what William should do to recover the slaves
and realise that value give an uncomfortable insight into Angus and his
times.

'Should think you might be able to trace Grace, and when you sell
Kitty McQuistin, which do to obtain stock, keep in view the high price
slaves will now be at. I do not know what you mean when you say Lucy
is useless, you do not say whether from age or ill-health. Rosy must be of
use when able to attend children. Use all diligences to get Mary Taaffe
and her two children back, as all the planters must turn their attention to
breeding slaves on their own estates. Try to secure Nancy Murphy from
further running away . . . Tom Murphy I would see to. (Presumably this
meant a whipping.) In one of your former letters you expressed that
doing away with the Slave Trade would be the ruin of Jamaica, and that
you might go to America or anywhere. I think a very little sound reason
will convince you that such property as mine will be bettered by it. Doing
away the Trade does not remove any part of your soil, your land is still
there, and as it is not a sugar or rum estate to require many to cultivate

canes, neither burthened with expensive machinery or stills, your slaves are sufficient for the utmost purpose you want . . . the law is not intended to alter the condition of those already possessed in any manner.'

Angus threatened William that if he could not fulfil his duty, and continued to withhold accounts, he would order him to find a purchaser for the Penn. William questioned whether Angus was legally entitled to sell the Penn, as the whole of the estate was still being wrapped up by the courts. This rankled Angus. His responses to repeated aspersions that he as yet had no title to the estate ranged from the hurtful to the hysterical. After two further packets arrived without news of William's grand plan, Angus finally lost all patience.

'It is a sweeping conclusion to tell me as I have not sown I might not expect to reap. If I have not sown, someone has for me, else that large quantity of land and number of slaves with other stock would not have been theirs. Am going to put many questions to you, and I beg they may be answered in the order in which they are put, without any evasion on your part . . . What reason can you justly give why you have withheld my accounts for four years, when they ought to have been transmitted half yearly or quarterly if required? How much coffee has the estate ever yielded? What did you sell it for? About how much land have you in coffee, in grass, and in untamed state? What did the coffee plants cost you? What does putting in grass cost per acre? How many People of Colour have you sold? What payment have you received for them? How have you applied that money? What livestock have you on the Penn? Not mentioning the slaves, those you have accounted for! How has Mayhew settled with you for Judy? (A reference to one of the McQuistin tribe who had stolen one of his slaves.) What sum do you annually pay for taxes, food, clothing, medicine and Medical attendance? . . . The conveyance is in the act of being made out to me of the Foreign Property, therefore I consider myself in full power now, but from your obstinacy in withholding from me the necessary information, I am not capable to judge whither it is most my interest to sell or keep the property . . . you have so disgusted me with your studied silence and by your little pitiful way of evading answers to the questions my interest leads me to ask!'

Two questions naturally arise. What was William doing on the property? And if he was in such desperate plight, why did Angus not jump on the first available ship to Jamaica and sort it out himself? Maria was no longer alive to restrain him, and though he wrote that it was his children which kept him at home, he did have Miss Burns as governess to look after them, and his sister only a few streets away. He may have been genuinely concerned about falling victim to tropical diseases, for he wrote in one letter to William, 'Say your opinion to my chance of keeping health were I to go out a month?' Naturally, he did not want his children to be fatherless as well as motherless. A voyage to the West Indies was a serious matter in those days, a long and dangerous journey from which many never returned.

The other possibility is that he wasn't as poor as he made out, that he was heavily gilding the lily. That year the final repayment on a sixteen-thousand-pound loan which Thomas McQuistin had made to another planter arrived from Jamaica, though with 'enormous legal deductions' which had Angus fervently writing to his attorney in Kingston, George Kinghorn, complaining bitterly that in his opinion five per cent was quite an adequate commission.

As to what William was doing on the Penn, a little imagination might take us a long way. In one letter, Angus accused him of being either drunk or stupid. Drunk and stupid he may have been. He may also have been pocketing every penny the property made.

In the summer of 1807, William seems to have allayed Angus' fears, for Angus, who had just returned from spending two months in Galloway with his father, wrote back,

'Your letter . . . appears most satisfactory. You now seem to be in a fair way, God contrive it. Although you have not been able to send me money, am most highly gratified to hear how you go on. In a little time, trust, you will be able to show yourself as one of the branches of our family . . .

Charles Angus, from a portrait painted probably before the trial. The artist is unknown, but it may have been Jeremiah Steele who was ultimately one of the witnesses against him.

Trinity Church and Trinity Place, a contemporary engraving. Trinity Place is the street immediately behind the church. To the right is King Street, where Alexander lived.
(With kind permission of the Liverpool Record Office)

Maria McQuistin, probably nine. Four years later she would become
Angus' wife.

A portrait of Charles Angus with his wife Maria and their three children.

Thomas McQuistin, slave owner from Jamaica, who became Angus'
father-in-law. His will caused a bitter feud.

Jane McQuistin, Margaret Burns' mother. Two of her husbands were slave owners, the third was the Keeper of the Royal Plate at St. James Place. She could have given evidence for the defence, but did not.

A contemporary sketch of Richard Statham who, as Town Clerk for Liverpool, mounted the prosecution against Charles Angus.
(With kind permission of the Liverpool Record Office)

The Crown Court at Lancaster Castle, where Angus was tried.
(From a guidebook, circa 1888, in the author's possession)

From your silence and want of accounts I had despaired that you had been one of us, now, I am glad you begin to show me the like kind of blood flows through your veins as if you spring from the same stock.'

There is no clearer example of Angus' humbug and pomposity than this. One wonders how much his father, the barber of Stranraer, forced him to change his tune. On the subject of good stock, Angus went on to say that when William would let him afford it, he would obtain for him a 'fine proven Maltese Ass, fifteen hands high' for which a Galloway farmer was asking a hundred guineas, but which Angus believed he could get for sixty. Angus must surely have wondered about the propriety of despatching yet another ass to St Faith's Penn.

There may well have been another reason why Angus did not want to leave his comfortable life in Liverpool and travel half way round the world to Jamaica. That reason involved Miss Burns herself. For by this time it seemed to many that she was looking after much more than just his domestic concerns.

6 'Uncommon Keen'

Around the start of the year 1807, a servant girl called Jane Overhin took the breakfast tray from the cook in the kitchen, and carried it upstairs to Angus' bedroom. She knocked on the door, but it was not Angus who answered. This was not the first time during her employment that Margaret Burns had answered that furtive knock. Jane Overhin did not go into the bedroom, as a servant most likely would have been required to do, but instead handed the tray to Margaret Burns at the door. If Jane Overhin is to be believed, she was a forward young woman for a servant, not afraid of speaking her mind, because she told the governess there and then that she thought she took great liberties, being in the master's bedroom so early in the morning. She then took an even more forward step and asked Miss Burns if they were to be married. Margaret Burns' answer is not recorded. She retired inside with the breakfast tray and shut the bedroom door, and Jane Overhin returned downstairs, no doubt to tittle tattle with the other servants about the disgustingly low moral standards at Trinity Place.

Jane Overhin wasn't the only servant to notice a 'liaison' between the master and the governess. A short while after she left his employment, another servant, Mary Peat, took up her duties at Trinity Place. Throughout her short service of only two to three months, Mary Peat was the only servant, cooking the meals, washing the pots and plates, lighting the fires, going errands, and cleaning the three-storey house from top to bottom. After a day's work, she probably deserved the sleep of the Gods. One night, however, she could not sleep, and lay in her small room at the top of the house, tossing and turning after a bad dream, frightened because she was alone. The moon was shining and it cast a ghostly pall on the furniture and walls. Mary Peat climbed out of bed, and padded downstairs to the children's room, in search of some feminine company.

In the bed lay the two girls, Jane and Maria, while sleeping soundly in the crib was little Thomas. But of Margaret Burns there was no sign. Mary Peat went back upstairs to her own room and put her head under the sheets, speculating on the whereabouts of the governess. She did not investigate further. (This was the story she would tell at the trial. There is every possibility that her nocturnal expedition had less to do with sleeplessness than with feminine curiosity.) In the morning, and on two or three other occasions, she noticed while making the bed that Margaret Burns' side had not been slept in.

The spirit of Sherlock Holmes, transported back into Georgian Liverpool, was now treading the elegant carpets of Number Two, Trinity Place.

In the evening, before going to bed, Mary Peat always took a brass candlestick and tinderbox into the parlour for the use of Miss Burns, who needed to light her way upstairs and see to the children before retiring. Usually she found the candlestick and tinderbox in the kitchen next morning, or occasionally on the stairs, but one morning she found them together on the table in Angus' bedroom. Just as one swallow does not make a summer, one candlestick does not make a liaison, but to the suspicious Mary Peat it was further confirmation that something was definitely going on.

This Holmesian spirit was not confined to the servants in Angus' employment. It burnt fiercely in the public-spirited breast of a fellow member of the Athenaeum, Henry Glover Moore. Glover Moore was also a merchant, who lived at Number 15, St Anne Street, only a minute's walk from Angus' house. They had known each other for about five years, and had walked to and from the Athenaeum together on many occasions. One night in the August of that year, Henry Glover Moore was returning home from a party along a route which took him by the side of Trinity Churchyard. It was between midnight and one in the morning, and the moon was shining brightly, just as it had been for Mary Peat. It must also have been a very balmy night, for Glover Moore noticed that the lower sash of Angus' parlour window was up, and that the blind was open. Living in the same area, he knew that the watchmen were pretty negligent (they were generally regarded as dull old fellows who in calling the hour nine times out of ten made a mistake) and thinking that someone had broken into Angus' house, decided to investigate.

The intrepid Henry Glover Moore did not proceed straight down Trinity Place towards the front of the house, but for some reason turned back and went down a passage that led from the rear of the house, until he came within four or five yards of the parlour window. What he claimed he saw, Angus would hotly dispute. Glover Moore first saw the hair of a person's head, realised it was Angus, but instead of passing on decided to linger, and saw, as he would describe it, 'Angus and Miss Burns sitting close together, his arm around her shoulder, their faces to each other, and that he was giving her a kiss'.

The incident was still fresh in his mind when, a few weeks later, he was strolling home from the Athenaeum with Angus. The conversation turned - as conversations with Angus seemed to do, according to his friends - upon the subject of unmarried women who had become pregnant. This time the matter came up regarding a young lady who had gone to the Isle of Man to have her child, and avoid public disgrace. Angus, according to Glover Moore, said that if she had come to him, he could have 'kissed' her (he was not sure if Angus actually used the word 'kissed') and that afterwards he could have got rid of her burden without her being so public a disgrace to her friends, and at less expense. If this was true, Angus was no longer dropping hints but admitting that he knew how to carry out abortions, and would be willing to do so for a discreet payment. At the time, being found guilty of giving an abortion carried the death penalty.

The lady from Liverpool who had gone to the Isle of Man came up again like the subject of some potentially awful limerick in Angus' conversation with James Cheyne, an insurance broker who lived in Daulby Street. Cheyne was not a member of the Athenaeum, but was waiting his turn for a share to become available. This time Angus said that the man who was guilty of such a thing had acted very improperly in having 'got the lady with child' but that he supposed it was possible to have given her something to 'carry it off'. Cheyne understood Angus to say that those things were generally done at so early a period 'that it was not supposed to have life'.

It is interesting to speculate on who this lady might have been. A few days before Christmas, Angus' brother Alexander in King Street suffered a 'violent derangement of mind' which was probably an epileptic seizure. He was thirty-two. The spring of the previous year he had fathered a bastard child by a girl living in Crosshall Street called Martha Williams, who was now pregnant with his second daughter. Angus rose to the occasion masterfully by conveying his unmarried brother on Christmas Eve to a private asylum fifty miles away near Blackburn, called the Billington Retreat. This peaceful haven, situated about one mile from the village of Whalley, in one of the most rural districts of Lancashire, had been established over thirty years before by the gloriously named Dr Abraham Chew as an asylum for the treatment of the insane, although it was known to locals simply as the Madhouse. There, patients underwent what was termed both medical and moral treatment. He would remain there for a year, under the care of Dr James Chew, the brother of the founder, and his assistant Ellis Chadwick.

There can be little doubt that by Christmas, speculation was rife that Margaret Burns was more than just looking after the needs of Angus' children. It wasn't just the servants' gossip, or the whispers in the smoke-filled coffee room at the Athenaeum. It was something altogether more visible. Margaret Burns was getting larger. This was noticeable to at least one of the local tradespeople with whom Miss Burns dealt. Mary Clarke kept a public house round the corner in King Street, and was accustomed to serving her with ale twice a day. Mary Clarke had nine children of her own, and felt well qualified to judge whether another woman was pregnant or not. To her eyes, and to those of her sister Alice Tellett who was living with her, her regular customer was definitely growing larger week by week. Later it would become obvious not only to the next-door neighbours, but to James Cheyne and the neighbourly Henry Glover Moore on their visits to Angus' house.

If Angus was aware of the growing tide of gossip, he certainly acted incautiously if the evidence of a portrait painter called Jeremiah

Steele is to be believed. Steele, who came from Nottingham, and who had already exhibited five miniatures at the Royal Academy of Art, was a guest one evening at the house of Dr Traill. Traill was a young Orkney man who had graduated in Edinburgh and had been practising in Liverpool for four years. He was a young and fashion-conscious member of Liverpool's small and provincial medical fraternity, living among the crème de la crème of Liverpool society in St Anne Street. It was a winter evening, and Steele was having supper with Traill, who had produced for their mutual interest a collection of books on anatomy, which contained a number of drawings of naked female figures. Doubtless these two gentlemen, one of the medical and one of the art world, had only the most professional regard for their subject. They were pouring over the illustrations when Angus arrived (invited or uninvited is not clear), and very soon the conversation turned - not, one may be relieved to hear, to the Lady from Liverpool - but to Angus' own medical knowledge, gained when he was a druggist's assistant and responsible for training young doctors to be surgeons aboard slave ships.

Traill must have winced. Here was one of his neighbours, who had never taken a degree of any kind in medicine, coming round to his house and boasting of sufficient knowledge to train others in the field. Angus said that in his early days in Liverpool he had taught several young men to be surgeons on slavers. Then he turned to the drawing of a dissection in the book - the dissection, as it happened, of a womb - and said that if he touched a certain part, namely the mouth of the womb, it would cause an abortion. According to Jeremiah Steele, Dr Traill looked up in astonishment. It was a secret, Traill said, given to him as a physician in a most secret way, that they were sworn never to use it except in a case of dire necessity, to save a patient's life.

Meanwhile, Margaret Burns continued to swell. It became increasingly noticeable to Angus' next-door neighbour at Number 3, Sarah Lawson. This lady would be a fairly minor witness at the trial, with no more to say than that Miss Burns appeared to give all the appearances of being pregnant, yet Angus would lay at her door much of the blame for his prosecution. So vitriolic was he when referring to her that her name was deleted from the published edition of the trial and she became that tantalising soubriquet, Mrs X. She was the wife of William Lawson, an agent to the Imperial Insurance Company, which had its offices at Bank Buildings, Castle Street, and had lived next door for about ten years. A woman, in Angus' words 'not of the most unspotted chastity', she was nevertheless in the habit of borrowing his crockery and other valuables to 'shine in' at her parties. Possibly she was envious of the Angus family crest which featured a crowned lion enclosed by a strap and buckle with the motto 'FORTIS EST VERITAS'. So fed up with his house being rarely free from her obtrusive borrowing, he gave orders to Miss Burns not to lend her anything else, but a row appears to have blown up over a basin of broken lumpsugar (it did not come refined in packets in those days) which Mrs Lawson had kept for a month without returning. Angus was for waiting to see just how long it would take her to return the sugar without being asked, but Miss Burns was determined not to lose it, and accordingly sent a servant next door for it. It was this act, and the like, which Angus claimed was one of the grand causes of Sarah Lawson's ill-mindedness. There was another cause, which Angus confided in a letter to his Kingston attorney, though strangely he kept it from his brother and nephew. Since he had become a widower, Angus wrote, Mrs Lawson had thrown out innumerable hints for him to become better acquainted with her, all of which he had rejected owing to the 'familiarity which subsisted between her and others in her husband's absence'. Customs and attitudes may change, but human nature remains inviolable.

About the middle of February, Angus walked into the druggist's shop of Steele and Oakes in Pool Lane (now South Castle Street) which was in the heart of the mercantile district and asked if they had any Oil of Savin. Oil of Savin is an irritant poison which comes from the leaves of a plant which grows extensively in country places. It is little known as a poison owing to its light yellow colour, its strong odour which resembles turpentine, and its hot burning taste. It is, however, better known as an abortive. Even an infusion of savin leaves, when drunk with the liquid, is extremely dangerous. It acts by throwing the uterus into a tetanic convulsion, and even a small overdose can cause great irritation and inflammation, whether applied to the skin or taken internally. The symptoms are excruciating pain, vomiting and diarrhoea, and often death.

John Steele the druggist knew Angus quite well as a customer and therefore had little compunction about selling it to him, as Oil of Savin could also be used as a medicine in the treatment of chlorosis, or 'green sickness', an iron-deficiency disorder common at that time among adolescent girls, or to treat abnormal absences of menstruation. Angus asked the price of it, and the druggist told him that Oil of Savin cost five shillings an ounce. This to Angus was far too expensive, and he made the point that if it had been cheaper he would have taken half an ounce. Two and sixpence was still expensive, however, so he agreed to take a quarter of an ounce and said that if it was good, it would probably answer his purpose. What his purpose was, Angus didn't say, and the druggist didn't ask. Angus handed over a phial with a cork in it, Steel weighed him two drachms of the oil (a quarter of a fluid ounce), poured it into the bottle, recorked it, and Angus left with his purchase.

Steele would see the bottle again, or at least a bottle very like it. He would say that the bottle was marked OL SAB, which is an abbreviation of the Latin name for the oil, Oleum Sabine. The inference would be that it was not the first time Angus had purchased such an item.

Angus' dislike of parting with small sums came to the fore again in what must be one of the most bizarre incidents in the whole story. About two weeks later he called at the shop of a cutler and surgeons' instrument maker which was owned by a Mr Thomas Richardson. Richardson had known Angus by sight for eight or nine years, and as a customer at a shop in which he had previously worked for a Mr Lloyd. Now that Richardson was set up on his own as a maker of surgical instruments, he was well acquainted with most if not all of the physicians and apothecaries in Liverpool.

Angus said that he wished to have an instrument sharpened, and produced a long tube, 'about ten inches long with a trocha, or three edged point'. If this sounds familiar, one should cast the mind back to the instrument he showed Peter Charnley. On that occasion, Angus made no secret of the fact it was designed for the purpose of causing a miscarriage. Now, here he was, asking for a very similar instrument to have its three-edged and dart-like point made 'uncommon keen'.

Richardson held the object and, rubbing his thumb over the point, told Angus that he could make it to answer his purposes better if he knew what the purposes were. Angus then explained that he wanted the instrument to bore his childrens' ears.

Richardson, who had made several instruments for the purpose of piercing ears, was taken aback. It was not unknown for young children to have their ears pierced or 'bored' for the purposes of being made to wear jewellery but the lobe of the ear was a delicate thing, and required a point more akin to a stocking needle. The object which he held in his hands would not just bore a hole in the ear but would tear it open. Nevertheless, the customer was always right (even then) for Richardson sharpened the instrument, and passed it back to Angus, who felt the point and said that he was very satisfied with it. Then came the thorny matter of the price. Richardson told Angus that it would cost him ninepence. At this Angus hesitated, and grumbled that in his opinion it was too much. Grudgingly, he paid up and left.

If Angus did want the Oil of Savin and the sharpened instrument to carry out an abortion on Miss Burns, it is astonishing that he should quibble about such small amounts of money. Both Steele and Richardson would remember his meanness.

That same week at the close of February, in which Angus walked home with his instrument made 'uncommon keen', two more servants came to take up employment at Trinity Place. Angus seems to have suffered from a high turnover of servants, or perhaps they just suffered from back-breaking work and poor wages. Betty Nickson was a young girl whose principal duties were to make the beds and clean the rooms. The other servant was a cook in her late forties called Ann Hopkins, a widow who had borne twelve children. Nickson and Hopkins would have good reason to wish they had taken employment elsewhere. Before March was out, their employment would be terminated abruptly, and with it the short and tragic life of Miss Margaret Burns.

7 Death of a Governess

By the beginning of March 1808, Miss Burns appeared to be in a very advanced state of pregnancy indeed. Angus' brother Alexander was still locked up in the private madhouse at Billington, his illegitimate and unbaptised child in the care of its mother who was now carrying his second. The scandalmongers of the district had plenty to wag their tongues about.

Around the first weekend of the month, Miss Burns paid a visit to her intimate friend, Elizabeth Jones, in Hunter Street. Since her own mother had now remarried and moved away, she was in the habit of consulting Elizabeth Jones' mother, Martha Barton, whenever she wanted medical advice of too delicate a nature for her to consult Angus. She complained to Mrs Barton that she was very ill, and irregular, and Mrs Barton recommended Welch's female pills. Unfortunately, Miss Burns had already tried Welch's pills for her 'condition', and they had done her no good. Mrs Barton then suggested that she try Grains of Paradise (the peppery seeds of an African aromatic plant) pounded up small in a glass of gin, a remedy that had cured her own daughter.

Welch's female pills was just one of the many proprietary 'female medicines' which were available at the time through newspaper advertisements, usually accompanied by the word LADIES in large letters in order to catch the eye. No hint was given as to the composition of the pills other than that they were composed of 'the best stomatick and anti-hysterical ingredients'. A century later, Welch's pills would still be going strong with a formula based solely on dried sulphate of iron, sulphur, powdered liquorice and turmeric, and maize starch. Thousands of women relied on these quack medicines when their periods became irregular or ceased altogether, and indeed the adverts often contained veiled recommendations that they could be used for cutting short an unwelcome pregnancy. Many were useless for that purpose, though some did contain irritants like savin and pennyroyal which were highly dangerous.

Whether the ailing Miss Burns ever resorted to the Grains of Paradise powdered up in gin, Mrs Barton never knew. It was the last time she would ever speak to her. About a week later, Miss Burns told her friend Elizabeth Jones that she was making preparations to return to her mother, just as soon as she had finished a piece of linen which she was embroidering. Her mother of course was now swanning round her apartment at St. James' Palace with her third husband, the Yeoman of the Silver Scullery, who with his salary of £136 per year plus a loaf of bread and a gallon of beer a day or money in lieu, had settled handsomely on her. A journey to London from Liverpool would entail thirty hours in a horse-drawn coach over rough ground, hardly an experience to be undertaken by a heavily pregnant woman.

It must have been an inordinately large piece of linen, because by the last week of March, Miss Burns was still in residence, though her duties no longer involved taking the children to Everton in the morning to fetch the milk and cream. This duty had been delegated to the new servant girl, Betty Nickson, who had taken the children for their early jaunt every morning since she arrived.

The 23rd of March, which was a Wednesday, dawned crisp and cold. (For an account of that day, and the subsequent two days, we have only the testimony of the two servants, Betty Nickson and Ann Hopkins. There is powerful evidence that both lied, and that both had good reason for lying). It was Ann Hopkins, the new cook, who had only been there about a month, who first noticed that Miss Burns rose early on that day. On entering the parlour, she saw the governess, who never usually got up until seven o'clock, go to a cupboard for something. The reason, Miss Burns said, was that she could not sleep. Having gone to the cupboard, Miss Burns then went into the hall, where she was seen climbing the stairs by Betty Nickson. An hour or so later at seven o'clock, the children were up and dressed, and Betty left the house with them to take them up the hill to Everton.

At the same time Angus left the house, and walked in the opposite direction, towards Church Street and the Athenaeum News Room. The most direct route lay southwards for a few yards down St. Anne Street, westwards along Folly Lane, then through the open hedge-lined grounds of the Seamen's Hospital and the Infirmary, dark red brick buildings with stone dressings, then past the largest building of all, the Lunatic Asylum, which had stood for nearly twenty years in a garden behind the Infirmary. The route would then take him across St. John's Lane and down past the northern extremity of the roperies, the long covered walkways where the rope was spun, and which, for as long as they existed, stopped any improvement in the neighbourhood. Finally, it was a short walk from the east side of the Theatre Royal to the Athenaeum. There, for the better part of an hour, Angus perused the *Liverpool Courier*, which had been established the previous year and which was published once a week on Wednesdays. In those days no London paper reached the provinces on the day of issue, and so the Courier carried national as well as local news, with the accent heavily on the former. Spain was the great centre of attention at the time, and the Courier contained many columns about the movements of Napoleon's armies.

By nine o'clock, Betty Nickson had returned from Everton, and Angus had come home for breakfast, which was served in the parlour for Angus, Miss Burns, and the three children. About a quarter past nine, Betty walked in to serve the family, and noticed that Miss Burns appeared to be very ill, so ill indeed that once breakfast was over she could scarcely walk across the room without leaning on a chair for support. Eventually she lay down on the sofa full length, complaining of violent pain in her bowels and extreme thirst.

Around ten o'clock, Miss Burns said she would like some water gruel to quench her dreadful thirst. Ann Hopkins made a pint of the stuff, and Betty took it into the parlour, but no sooner had the governess drunk it than it came up with her breakfast. The vomit according to Betty was very black. More gruel was made, and left by the fire all day for when she wanted some, but every time she drank it she vomited it up almost immediately. She continued in this way for the rest of the day, lying on the sofa in continual pain, drinking water gruel but throwing it up. All in all, she consumed about three quarts. She was so unwell that she could not even walk or sit up, for it was painful to be on her feet. Neither could she bear to be touched.

Meanwhile, Betty Nickson was in and out of the parlour, removing the sick bowl, and observed that whereas at first the vomit had been black, it now took on a greenish colour. Ann Hopkins noticed that there was something in it which resembled the yolk of an egg, or the inside of an orange. Angus never left the house for the rest of that day, and much of the time he spent with Miss Burns in the parlour, where a fire was kept up constantly. Nothing appears to have been said, at least on that day, either by Angus, Miss Burns or the two servants, about calling in a doctor.

In the evening, Ann Hopkins asked Miss Burns if she and Betty Nickson should bring their bed down into her room, and make a fire there, but Miss Burns told them not to bother. Mr. Angus, she said, would sit up with her, as he had been accustomed to sitting up with his wife when she was ill. Betty also asked, but Angus said to her 'No, no, Betty, you go to bed, you have work to do tomorrow'. Their offer having been refused, they went upstairs and brought down an easy chair together, then Betty brought down separately a quilt and two pillows.

Having made Miss Burns comfortable for the night, the servants retired to bed about ten o'clock, and had no cause to get up again until six on the Thursday morning. Upon rising, Ann Hopkins went into the parlour, followed straightaway by Betty Nickson. Miss Burns was still lying on the sofa with the pillows under her head, in terrible pain, complaining of the most violent thirst. Angus was in the easychair, but almost as soon as the servants came in he went upstairs to bed, where he remained until nine. Possibly he had spent an uncomfortable night and wished to catch up on sleep. While he was in bed, Ann Hopkins cleaned about the parlour. Miss Burns said she was tired of gruel, and the cook asked her if she had any buttermilk in the house. There being none, Ann Hopkins went out to get her some, and on returning made her a water-posset, which she drank. It was not long on her stomach when she vomited that up. This time the vomit was even blacker than it had been the day before.

When Angus came down for breakfast, Miss Burns was no better. She asked for some warm beer, which Betty Nickson heated up herself, but that too was vomited up. Miss Burns was also by now 'badly hurt to make water', so the cook went into the kitchen, sliced up an onion, and poured some boiling water on top of it. Miss Burns sat on the onion and claimed that it gave her some relief, but she still continued sick all the day.

It was now that a doctor was first mentioned, and here Ann Hopkins and Betty Nickson would differ about exactly what was said. According to the young servant girl, it was at eleven o'clock that morning when Angus suggested sending for the family doctor, Henry Park, telling Miss Burns that she should not be afraid of the expense. Miss Burns turned down the offer, and in a light, indifferent tone replied 'No, no, Mr Angus, tutt, tutt, they (doctors) can do me no good'.

According to Ann Hopkins, however, Miss Burns told her during the course of the day that Angus was going out to a doctor to advise about her. Clearly both accounts could not be true. Wherever the truth lay, no doctor came, that day or the next. Angus did go out a little before dinner, but it was to visit his brother-in-law William Biggam, leaving Miss Burns in the capable hands of the two servants. Still she was throwing up everything which touched her stomach. At one stage, after retching violently, she turned to Betty and exclaimed 'Oh Betty, what bile comes off my stomach - I wish I had taken an emetic long since!' In the circumstances, this seems an extraordinary thing for her to say. One would have thought that by this time she would be so dehydrated and exhausted by constant vomiting that the last thing on her mind would be an emetic.

Angus returned from the Biggams' about quarter to three that afternoon. Miss Burns was no better. The pains in her body were still so severe that she could not put her feet to the ground, and from time to time she had to hold fast with her hands to the end of the sofa. Her thirst was almost unquenchable.

Betty Nickson would testify at the trial that there was some respite from the vomiting on the Thursday evening, and that Miss Burns could 'stir more about'. But by bedtime, Angus was planning to sit up with her for a second night, and refusing the servants' offer to sit up instead. This time he said he could not sleep anyway, because of the agitation of mind he was suffering on account of his brother Alexander's mental derangement. Just before ten, Miss Burns asked Betty to bring her down a clean bedgown, which the servant did. Then both servants went to bed, leaving Angus reading in the parlour, and Miss Burns weak and exhausted on the sofa.

At four o'clock on the Friday morning, the bell rang in Betty Nickson's room. She rose and came downstairs to be told by Angus that she should attend to the children, as they were crying. Miss Burns was still stretched out on the sofa, and appeared to be much worse. Her breathing was very quick. Either before or after she attended to the children, she fetched Angus a pint jug of cold water from the kitchen, then went back to bed to catch what sleep she could before getting up again at six.

When Betty and Ann Hopkins entered the parlour shortly after six on the Friday morning, Angus was in his easychair (the servants would differ in their testimony as to whether he was sitting or sleeping) and Miss Burns was still lying on the sofa, feeling much better as the pain had left her, though the vomiting had given way to a bad bout of diarrhoea. Miss Burns asked for some warm beer, which Ann Hopkins drew and heated up, and this seemed to settle her stomach. Later on, she even took a bowlful of gruel, and this too settled. By ten, Miss Burns must have made a miraculous recovery, because she now felt like some white wine, and asked Betty to go out to Mr Winstanley's, a wine merchant in Henry Street, and purchase two bottles. Betty had a bad foot that morning from a sprain, and had already limped to Everton and back. Now she was expected to walk to Henry Street, which was practically at the other side of Liverpool, well beyond the Athenaeum.

Miss Burns' recovery was now boundless. No sooner had Betty left the house and gone for the wine, than Ann Hopkins was called into the parlour to take an order for dinner, and also to receive instructions to make some barley water. Ann Hopkins went downstairs to the kitchen to prepare the barley water and the dinner, and did not go back into the parlour until Betty returned.

At about quarter past eleven, Betty Nickson arrived back at Trinity Place with the two bottles of wine, having been absent from the house for the space of an hour and ten minutes. By her own evidence, she had had some trouble in finding Mr Winstanley and getting him to unlock the shop, and that, plus her sprained foot, had caused her to be such a long time. She went straight into the parlour, noticing that the chamber pot was behind the door, and that the action of her opening the door propelled it into the centre of the room. She got such a fright at what she saw that she raced downstairs to the kitchen and asked the cook where Miss Burns was, as she could not at first believe the evidence of her eyes. Ann Hopkins, who had only been out of the parlour less than half an hour, went up with Betty, and this time they entered together.

Poor Margaret Burns. Nothing became her life so much as her manner of leaving it. When the servants stepped into the parlour, the governess was cowered in a lump in a corner of the room, her elbows on her knees, and her face pressed against the wall. She was dead. What made the scene so bizarre, so inexplicable, was that less than half an hour after ordering dinner, Charles Angus had the quilt pulled over him on his easychair, and was fast asleep.

8 Enemies and Neighbours

It took some considerable time for the servants to wake Angus. Betty Nickson was screaming, and the cook was shaking him by the shoulders, but he seemed to be in such a deep sleep that it was some moments before they managed to rouse him. When finally he did open his eyes, he threw off the quilt and jumped up into the middle of the parlour, and said, 'Good God, what's this?' Betty Nickson answered 'She's dead, she's dead!' and Angus cried out 'Good God, poor Margaret'. For a few minutes, according to the servants, they stood around as though not knowing quite what to do. Then Ann Hopkins suggested to Angus that they lift her up and lie her on the sofa, and asked if Angus would help. Angus did so, and he and the cook lifted her up and stretched her out on the sofa, on her back, on top of Angus' flannel morning gown. Then Angus asked if Betty would go and fetch his sister, Mrs Biggam.

Betty left the house for the third time on that chilly morning, crossed St. Anne Street, and made her way to the Biggams' house which was in the direction of the river. Both the Biggams were in, and they returned to Trinity Place with the servant, William Biggam going via Hunter Street to break the news to Miss Burns' close friend Elizabeth Jones, who also joined the party heading towards Trinity Place.

By shortly after noon, there were seven people milling about the corpse of Margaret Burns. Angus, his two servants, the Biggams and Elizabeth Jones had now been joined by Angus' brother's servant from round the corner. Her name is not recorded, but she must have been looking after the house while her master was 'recovering' in the asylum. Ann Hopkins, Mrs Biggam and Elizabeth Jones proceeded to strip the body of clothes, removing from it the bedgown which had been brought down the night before, a waistcoat and petticoat also made of flannel, her shift and her cotton stockings. Most of these items would later be described as wet and bloody by the constable who eventually took them, while Ann Hopkins would only say that the shift had the appearance of blood on it. Underneath, two cloths were found, fastened as bandages round her thighs by a piece of tape, and these too were removed. Ann Hopkins then took all of the clothes, including the 'bandages', down into the cellar. Some mystery would revolve around Miss Burns' stays. Betty Nickson would say that in the course of the morning she had found them on the floor in the nursery, and that she had no idea who had put them there, though later she would agree that she may in the confusion have placed them there herself.

There was now the little problem of the body. Incredibly, not one of the seven people in the house on that Friday afternoon saw fit to fetch a doctor to examine it. Instead, the five women, Ann Hopkins, Betty Nickson, Mrs Biggam, Elizabeth Jones and the servant from King Street all lifted the corpse of Miss Burns and carried it upstairs to the bedroom which was directly above the parlour, and there they laid it out on the bed.

There was yet another visitor to the house that day who saw the body and did nothing about it. This was Betty Nickson's mother, Jane Nickson. Like so many of the women whose evidence would mount against Angus, she had borne a large brood of children. She had visited the house from time to time since her daughter took up employment there, and had seen Miss Burns on two occasions. Now, on that Friday, she arrived to find the house in turmoil. A plate of salt was placed on the corpse. It was a widespread superstition that salt not only kept away evil spirits but was believed to prevent the body from swelling.

Gradually the house emptied of visitors until there was only Mrs Biggam, Angus' sister, left. She remained for the whole of the day and into the early hours of Saturday morning, long after the servants had gone to bed. Finally, between two and three a.m., she took her leave, and Angus himself retired. One wonders what they talked about, and how soundly the household slept. Stillest of all was Miss Burns, the dish of salt laid upon her, the window of her room almost certainly wide open to allow her soul to freely depart. There was nothing unusual in a body lying around the house for days after a death, until the coroner's jury came to examine it. Luckily, the weather was cold that night, and would remain so for some time.

A little after eight o'clock on the morning of Saturday the 26th, Angus rose, and at nine o'clock the washerwoman called round to collect the clothes for washing. It is unclear whether Saturday morning was her usual time of calling, or whether she had been asked specially to come. Betty Nickson counted the clothes in the parlour, while Angus wrote down an account of them in his fastidious way. According to Betty Nickson, only four items were given to the washerwoman, a bedgown and petticoat which were stained with vomit, and a muslin cap and a pair of stockings. The bedgown was presumably the old one, and not the bloody one she had been wearing when she died.

For the whole of that day, and all of Saturday night, the corpse lay upstairs and still no doctor was called to examine it. By the Sunday morning, it had lain there nearly forty-eight hours. Reports were circulating however, and it clearly could not lie unattended for much longer. Neither could Angus have been aware of the tide that was turning against him. It must only have been a matter of how long, like King Canute, he could hold it back. Exactly who informed the coroner isn't known, but Angus had few doubts. He attributed it to his next-door neighbour, Sarah Lawson, who had probably witnessed the comings and goings and listened to the servants' gossip. At his trial, Angus would describe her as a woman moved by the need to 'gratify curiosity and promote slander'. However it happened, on that Sunday morning the waves of the unstemmed tide finally broke, and the coroner of Liverpool, Thomas Molyneaux, sent a note to Dr. Rutter, the senior medical examiner of the town, asking him to go to Trinity Place and conduct an examination of the body. In turn, Dr. Rutter sent a note by hand round to Angus' house, informing him of his intention to visit.

There was, of course, no police force worthy of the name to undertake an enquiry into a suspicious death. What police there were had been established under the provisions of 'An act for building a church in the town of Liverpool, in the County of Palatine of Lancaster, and for enlightening and cleansing the streets of the said town, and for keeping and maintaining a Nightly Watch there'. Most of them were lamentably inefficient, wheezy and asthmatic old men who laboured under great coats and immense capes, and were frequently the butt of practical jokes, such as the practise of nailing them in their boxes while they were asleep. It will be easily understood that the investigation of a crime, particularly when it was a domestic affair involving one of the higher classes, was a pretty leisurely affair.

The doctor's visit, obligingly announced beforehand, was preceded by the arrival of another gentleman who was to play a prominent role in the case. This was the Reverend John Vause, the incumbent of Christ Church, a fashionable place of worship in Hunter Street. A near neighbour of Angus', and a fellow member of the Athenaeum, he had known Angus for more than nine years. Vause was thirty-eight years old, the son of a Wigan clergyman, and had been a pupil at Eton until the age of eighteen, after which he had matriculated at King's College, Cambridge. He had been ordained to the Anglican priesthood in Norwich, returned to Eton as a master, and in 1800 been appointed minister of the newly consecrated Christ Church, described at the time as being commodious and lofty, and possessing a certain air of dignity. Unfortunately no such loftiness or dignity attached itself to the character of John Vause. Although he had been married for eight years, his moral reputation in the town did not stand up. Reckoned to be a brilliant star in the pulpit with an effective style, voice and manner, he led a life which as one commentator put it 'unhappily contradicted and marred all of his Sunday school teachings'. A leading Tory, he would be satirised in the same election pamphlet that gave Richard Statham an ass called Allbum by being given one called Lechery, much to the robust merriment of his friends. As such, he was in no position to question Angus' morals.

Vause asked him when the unfortunate incident had taken place, and Angus said 'On Saturday'. Vause was surprised at this as it was his understanding that Miss Burns had died on the Friday, not the Saturday. What fixed the Friday in his mind was the fact that on the Friday morning between seven and eight o'clock, he had been to the Athenaeum and had walked home with Angus. This Angus would hotly deny, for reasons that will emerge. He immediately rang the bell and Betty Nickson came in. Angus asked her on what morning Miss Burns had died, and Betty answered truthfully that it was definitely on the Friday. With that she was dismissed, and Angus justified his lapse of memory by saying that he was so bewildered and bedevilled that he didn't know what had come over him. Being 'bewildered and bedevilled' was a favourite expression of Angus', which Vause had heard him use many times before.

Vause asked about the story gaining currency that Miss Burns had given birth to a child. Angus' answer, if Vause remembered correctly, was that 'he had not any idea she was with-child'. This of course could be taken two ways. Either Miss Burns had had a child, and Angus had not been aware until the birth that she had been pregnant. Or she had not had a child at all. Vause accepted the latter. Angus went on to explain that she had suffered from a violent vomiting and bowel complaint, to which Vause suggested that she might have been 'quacking' herself, or taking some improper medicine as he knew that Angus kept a medicine chest in his house. Angus said that could not be, that he had given her medicine himself - seven drops of laudanum one night, and ten drops of laudanum another, though he did not say on which nights. In the same breath he also told the clergyman she had a black puke. This phrase was to rebound and cause great confusion out of all proportion to its meaning. Angus meant that the stomach contents which she had vomited up had been black, but Vause seemed to think that Angus was admitting to giving her a medicine called a black puke. The confusion is understandable when one considers that the word puke in those days was also used to describe an emetic, or any medicine that excited vomiting. What is harder to fathom is how this simple misunderstanding wasn't nipped at the source. The black puke would come up again, when it would be elevated to the status of a sinister and deadly poison.

Vause left, seemingly reassured, to vindicate Angus' character in the world, or at least in Liverpool. He would return before the day was out. Now it was the turn of the good doctors of Liverpool to invade Number Two, Trinity Place, to try and solve the mystery of the death of Margaret Burns.

9 The Corpse is Opened

Dr. John Rutter had a dilemma. He was a Quaker. As such he was concerned that if his visit to Trinity Place was to lead to criminal proceedings he would be unable to give evidence, the reason being that he could not take the oath. It was because of this that the forty-six-year-old doctor, one of the founders of the Athenaeum and regarded as the head of the medical profession in Liverpool, decided to take some medical colleagues with him.

Before giving an account of how these medical gentlemen examined the dead, it may be informative to produce a solitary example of how the living were treated in those early days of the nineteenth century. A record exists of the daily treatment of one of Dr. Rutter's patients who had a high fever, bad cough, pain in her side, and difficulty breathing. Dr. Rutter ordered her to be put in warm water and to take antimonial wine, then,

Feb. 27	Emetic
March 3	Emetic
March 6	Eruption full out
March 7	Put in warm water
March 8	Leeches applied twice to foot.
	Vinegar of squills, blister on back.
March 10	So bad, doctor called four times.
	Given strawberries, James Powder,
	warm water poured over her feet, and
	hands and feet bathed with vinegar.
	Got worse.

After more days of sponging and leeches,

March 18	Strawberries : Emetic
March 19	Very ill indeed
March 23	Calomel : Laudanum

March 24	Carried in coach to Greenbank
March 25	Not one hope of her recovery
March 26	Carried into garden
March 30	Cream and Gravey (sic). No doctor today.
	(She got better)

One should not of course criticise the traditions and customs of preceding ages. Liverpool in 1808 was the home of a small and provincial medical school, composed of many men of vision. As well as the Infirmary, the town boasted a charitable Dispensary, set up to help remedy the neglected state of the poor of the parish in cases of sickness. It stood next door to the Athenaeum in Church Street, with a tablet built into the wall containing a bas-relief of the Good Samaritan.

Of the three medical men which Dr. Rutter asked to accompany him, Dr. James Gerard was the most experienced. He had been one of the first surgeons appointed to the Dispensary when it opened thirty years before. Lately, up until the year of abolition, he had sat on the Board of Examiners at the Infirmary testing and certifying would-be surgeons for service on slave ships. Gerard was a great idol of the ladies, especially with the hostesses of St. Anne Street, and would graciously accept all their invitations to their female gatherings or 'routs' as they were called. In that capacity, it is quite likely he had been the honoured male guest at Sarah Lawson's parties, eating off Angus' borrowed crockery on many an occasion.

The others were Thomas Fairfax Hay, a surgeon-apothecary, and another young surgeon Thomas Christian. Christian had to go out of town on business the same day, and though he came to the house, played little part in the future proceedings. Fairfax Hay took with him an apprentice called George Robinson. The term surgeon-apothecary sounds odd today, but in practice it meant just that. Apothecaries, who had invaded the practice of 'physic', were totally without qualifications or formal training, unlike the physicians who had some tuition in anatomy. This bizarre anomaly would not be rectified for five decades.

It is ironic that Miss Burns, who so distrusted medical men, should suddenly have become the object of attention for five of them.

Rutter, Gerard, Fairfax Hay and Robinson all turned up at Trinity Place at two o'clock on Sunday afternoon (Christian would arrive later) where they were introduced into the parlour. There, Rutter presented to Angus another note, this one from the coroner as the authority under which they had come. Angus spent a few moments perusing the note and then told the medical party that he was perfectly willing for them to make an examination. Ann Hopkins the cook then led the gentlemen upstairs, and into the bedroom in which the corpse had now lain for fifty hours. It was dressed in a shift, and was still in a very good state of preservation.

Gerard asked the cook how long Miss Burns had been ill and Ann Hopkins answered two days, saying that she had died on Friday the 25th at a quarter past eleven in the morning. She had been affected with looseness and sickness, but with no other complaint.

The party lifted the body off the bed, observing a small stain of blood on the sheet, and some fluid that had seeped from the head onto the pillow. No sooner was it laid on the table in the room and the shift pulled up over the head, when a quantity of thin yellowish fluid poured from the nostrils, and this was collected for future examination. A preliminary investigation established that there were no marks of external violence on the body. The nails of the fingers were of a bluish colour, and the veins on the surface of the abdomen appeared very enlarged.

Out came the anatomical knives, and upon the bedroom table the abdomen of Miss Burns was cut open. Inside they found a considerable quantity of dark olive-coloured fluid that they would claim before the coroner had an acrid smell similar to that which issued from the nostrils. A number of large globules of a dark-coloured, dense, oily fluid floated upon this, but of no particular odour. On the external coat of parts of the small intestines they found inflamation marks though the large intestines were free of them. Also inflamed were a part of the curvature of the stomach and a small portion of the anterior edge of the liver which was directly over it. They then raised up the stomach bag, and discovered in what they would call 'the anterior and inferior part of its great curvature' a hole through which the quantity of dark, olive-coloured fluid had issued. Of this, some fluid ounces were collected and preserved for further examination. The stomach itself contained about a pint of the fluid. The natural structure of the lining of the stomach for a considerable area around the opening was destroyed, and the whole area was so soft, pulpy and tender that Fairfax Hay would later admit that in moving the stomach he accidentally stuck his fingers through it and enlarged the hole, which had in its original state been nearly the size of a crown piece. There was, however, no inflamation around the hole. They then set about removing the stomach from the body, and having done so they washed out the inner surface and preserved the washed out contents. A quantity, about three ounces, of a fluid resembling that in the stomach, but not quite so thick, was also taken out of one of the small intestines and preserved.

The medical gentlemen then turned their attention to the womb. They found it considerably enlarged, and on the inner surface of the uterus, plainly discernible, was a rugged circular mark about four inches in diameter to which, in their opinion, a placenta had adhered. The mouth of the uterus was greatly dilated, and the hole was, in Fairfax Hay's words, the 'size of a bullock's heart'. Not only that, but the vessels going from the uterus to the placenta for the nourishment of a child were quite visible. Not one of them had any doubt that Margaret Burns had recently given birth to an almost fully grown baby.

Meanwhile, Angus waited in the parlour, listening to the footsteps in the room overhead as the body was dissected. Between two and three o'clock, he received a second visit from the Reverend John Vause. Ann Hopkins came in to brush the hearth, and as she did so muttered that they were making too much of it, that it was quite needless. Vause became indignant at the remark. He told her candidly that nothing could be needless when the 'innocence and honour of her master were so nearly and tenderly concerned'. Angus, for his part, was now anxious to stress that on the Friday morning when Miss Burns had been suffering from diarrhoea, he had left the room seven or eight times out of delicacy 'whenever it was necessary' so that she could use the chamber pot, and in this the cook backed him up. Angus seemed eager for the cook to tell Vause everything she knew, and to Vause she described Miss Burns' excessive thirst, and the fact that she had asked for some beer. (Ann Hopkins hadn't mentioned the excessive thirst to the doctors.)

Vause wondered whether she thought it proper to give her beer at that time of the morning, and it was now Ann Hopkins' turn to be indignant, answering that she had given her beer and plenty of gruel besides. For her own part, the cook told the clergyman, she never thought the governess so very ill. Betty Nickson had thought Miss Burns would never get better, but she thought otherwise. And with that, Ann Hopkins left the room.

If Vause had suspicions that Angus had left the room 'when necessary' for other reasons than to let Miss Burns use the chamber pot, he was keeping them very close to his chest. Angus finally came up with a theory to explain her death, and the other mysterious circumstances. She had been alone with him, he said, when she badly needed to use the chamber pot. Seeing that he was asleep in his chair, and not wishing to disturb him, she was going from delicacy into the other parlour, when she must have died of a sudden fit. That, Angus explained, was how the chamber pot came to be behind the door. Her complaint, he now stressed, was the fluor albus, under which she had 'long laboured' and which had weakened her excessively. (Fluor Albus, meaning literally 'white fluid' was the old name for whites, a whitish or yellowish discharge of mucus from the vagina, also known as leucorrhea. In most cases it occurs naturally and does not signify any disorder, but if copious, the discharge may be a symptom of vaginal infection. It is hard to see how it could lead to a fit, though to be fair, Angus may not have intended any connection).

Vause left before the doctors finished their examination. About four o'clock Rutter, Gerard, Fairfax Hay, Robinson and Christian came downstairs with the stomach and uterus of Miss Burns in separate vessels, and other vessels containing the various fluids from the stomach, intestines and abdominal cavity, as well as that which had issued earlier from her nostrils. They told Angus that they were taking them for examination, and left the house, without delay. Upstairs, what remained of Miss Burns lay cut up on the bedroom table, a hollowed out carcass.

In the columns of the local newspaper, the death of a governess, even one who was possibly a victim of murder, did not get so much as a passing mention.

The investigation now gathered pace with almost reckless haste. Neither Rutter, Gerard or Fairfax Hay were analytical chemists, capable of subjecting the stomach contents and other fluids to the tests which were deemed sufficient in those days to establish the existence of poison. That some kind of corrosive poison had caused the hole in Margaret Burns' stomach seemed a strong possibility. The problem was, which poison?

For the answer, they turned to another of their medical colleagues, Dr. John Bostock. In his mid-thirties, Bostock was a physician with some expertise in the relatively new field of scientific chemistry. He had been only one year old when his father, also a physician, had died, and Bostock had followed in his footsteps, first studying medicine under the care of a Liverpool apothecary and then going on to be a student at Edinburgh. After studying anatomy in London, at the height of the resurrection trade when graves were robbed and freshly buried corpses hawked for research and teaching purposes, he had finally returned to Liverpool to become physician to the Dispensary.

Bostock went at first to Dr. Rutter's, and from there accompanied Fairfax Hay to his house, where the uterus and stomach of Miss Burns were now preserved in spirit, alongside the various vessels of yellowish and olive green body fluids. Bostock studied the uterus and concurred with his colleagues' opinions that there was no other explanation for its dilated size than that it had recently expelled a fully grown foetus. He was shown the stomach, and the ragged hole which Fairfax Hay had accidentally enlarged with his fingers. To him, it was not so much ragged, as pulpy and tender. He agreed with his colleagues that a possible explanation was that a corrosive poison had been introduced into the stomach, but on this they were much more guarded than on the matter of the uterus.

Bostock took the various vessels of fluids back to his house to commence experimentation, in the presence of both Dr. Rutter and Dr.

Gerard. These vessels contained the separate fluids from the nose, the stomach, the small intestines, and the washed-out contents of the stomach bag, a fact worth remembering since at the trial only two of them would merit a mention. Their first action was to sniff the contents of the stomach to see if their collective noses could detect any known vegetable poison, such as savin. They drew a blank. They next turned their attention to the metallic irritant as well as the corrosive poisons, the most well known and widely used of the irritant poisons being of course arsenic. Unfortunately, in 1808, there were no reliable scientific tests for arsenic. It would be another twenty eight years before the great breakthrough would be made by an English chemist, James Marsh, who in a test named after him made it possible to detect as little as a fiftieth of a milligram. Until Marsh's discovery, experiments to find arsenic in solutions containing organic matter depended largely on the colour of precipitate produced when the solution was mixed with a little carbonate of potash, and sulphate of copper or nitrate of silver added.

Failing to find any traces of poison in the stomach, they turned their attention to the intestinal and other fluids. As with the contents of the stomach, they could find no evidence of poison. What is astonishing is that since a corrosive or metallic irritant poison was suspected, they never examined the gullet to see if there were any signs of it having been swallowed. Neither would that be their only shortcoming.

Their experiments, however, had only just begun. It would later be levelled at them that 'from the days of Hippocrates to the present time, there never was a more deficient, unprofessional dissection on which any important consequences depended, than that of the body of this lady'. How deficient it was we shall see. The storm that would rock the medical fraternity of Liverpool and ruffle many a reputation was about to break.

Meanwhile, the port was awash with rumour and speculation. Up and down St. Anne Street, in the mansions of the wealthy and the wise, the talk was of nothing else. Hurrying to evening service on that chilly Sunday night, the merchants of the town were less concerned with their eventual salvation than they were with what had transpired inside Angus' house. Murder among the poorer classes excited no comment, but Angus was a member of the Athenaeum, a neighbour, a respectable merchant. The prejudice against him was already running high. The fact has to be faced that it may in part have had something to do with his nationality. The success of Scots in business brought many a jeer from southerners, and encouraged many a lampoon. It would have been unthinkable to have put on the stage or in any satire a Scotsman who was not pawky or mean-hearted - as unthinkable as portraying a jew without his long red beard and desire for his pound of flesh. Sir Pertinax MacSycophant of Macklin's *Man of the World*, and Sir Archy Macsarcasm in *Love à la Mode* were regarded as wonderfully accurate portraits of the typical inhabitant of North Britain. The deep unpopularity of Lord Bute, the one-time prime minister and personal favourite of George the Third, was more owing to his being a Scotsman than to his incompetency. And when a Scots regiment had been called out to quell a riot in London, it was seen as the ultimate affront to national dignity. It would be remarkable then if Angus' profitable marriage to young Maria and subsequent disastrous business enterprise hadn't earned him a few curls of the lip and scornful sneers.

On Monday, the 28th of March, the inquest opened at the new Liverpool Exchange in Castle Street. The building had only just been opened that month, after a demand from the upper echelons of the commercial community for better accommodation in which to transact business. On this Monday, the crowd was thick, but not for the purposes of discussing business. This time they had come to listen to the evidence, such as it was, against one of their own. The jury would be composed of people who either knew Angus or knew of him. A number of them were undoubtedly members of the Athenaeum.

Allowed no time to arrange legal representation for himself, Angus was at the mercy of the Clerk to the Coroner, whose responsibility it was to summon the witnesses. Under the governing charter of the port, the position of Clerk to the Coroner was embraced by the Town Clerk, who rather incestuously filled the roles of Clerk to the Mayor's Court, Clerk of the Peace for the Borough, and Clerk to the Magistrates, as well as legal adviser to the Mayor. The present Town Clerk also happened to be the solicitor to the corporation, which meant that in the event of Angus being sent for trial, he would almost certainly bid to become solicitor for the prosecution.

It was Angus' bad fortune that the proud bearer of all of those titles in 1808 happened to be his most inveterate enemy, Richard Statham.

❦ ❦ ❦

10 A Solicitor's Revenge

'My being brought here has been more to gratify private revenge and malicious enmity, than from any knowledge of me having done wrong, or a desire to promote the ends of public justice. Mr Statham, the Town Clerk of Liverpool, and Mrs Sarah Lawson, I shall ever consider the instigators of this prosecution.'

So Angus would say at his trial. He may have had a point. The Town Council, or Common Council as it was known, was in those days a self-elected body which perpetuated the keeping of the municipal affairs of the town in the hands of just a few families, a state of affairs that inevitably led to corruption and gave rise to the feeling that there was a singular lack of talent in charge. Richard Statham was not the most brilliant Town Clerk of the period - indeed he appears to have been a figure of fun - but he was that most dangerous of creatures, a man in a position of power who also bore a longstanding grudge. Statham had never forgiven Angus for preventing him from being the executor of his father-in-law's will. Consequently, Angus would accuse Statham of interfering with the testimony of witnesses at the inquest, of bullying them to say what he wanted them to say, of turning his own servants against him, and of setting out not only to ruin his reputation but to have his life taken away on the gallows.

As for Sarah Lawson, it is hard to imagine that her thirst for enmity was the result of a sole request to return a basin of broken lumpsugar. Nevertheless, she had spent the previous day, and would spend much of the period of the inquest scouring Liverpool for every servant who had ever worked for Angus, and who could testify as to the relationship between him and Miss Burns. Inevitably she came up with Jane Overhin (who had the breakfast tray taken from her at the bedroom door) and Mary Peat (the unslept-in bed and the tell-tale candlestick). As the redoubtable next-door neighbour would be accused by Angus of gratifying curiosity and promoting slander, it is worth considering that she may well have been a woman, 'not of unspotted chastity', whose sexual advances Angus had turned down.

No verbatim account of the inquest survives, but from other sources it is possible to piece together the more important proceedings. The first duty of the jury was to view the body. This grisly procedure, then governed by statute, no doubt turned the stomach of many a hardened citizen, and encouraged him to make up his mind before even a word of evidence had been heard. The jurors were taken the half mile to Trinity Place, where they tramped upstairs to the bedroom over the parlour and were shown the corpse of Miss Burns. Whether it had been removed from the table to the bed, or whether it was now in a coffin, is not recorded - but the fact that it was without stomach or uterus, the two organs on which their intellects would be taxed, mattered little. Having done what was required of them, they filed back downstairs and returned to the Exchange.

The inquest lasted from Monday the 28th of March until Friday 1st of April. The medical men - Rutter, Gerard, Bostock and Fairfax Hay - had already informally stated their findings to the coroner the day before, conveying their belief that Miss Burns had died after giving birth to an almost fully grown child, along with their suspicion that the cause of death had been the swallowing of some corrosive poison. Their full report would not be written up until the Wednesday, when they would give their depositions. In the mean time, there were plenty of witnesses to examine, starting with Elizabeth Nickson and Ann Hopkins.

Most damaging was their testimony that on the morning Miss Burns died, they had encountered great trouble in waking Angus, that they were obliged to literally shake him out of his chair. There could hardly have been one person at the inquest who was not impressed by those mysterious circumstances. Angus' movements on the three days were also minutely examined. The servants spoke of how, on the Wednesday, he had gone to the Athenaeum to read the newspapers, and how, on the Thursday, he had gone out a little before dinner to visit his brother-in-law, and returned just after three o'clock. He was not out at all, however, on the Friday morning that Miss Burns died, nor was he out for the remainder of that day. This fact would take on immense importance at the trial. At this stage, it is worth remembering that only the servants claimed to have left the house on the Friday morning, Ann Hopkins to buy the buttermilk, and Betty Nickson to fetch the two bottles of wine from Mr Winstanley's in Henry Street. It was during Betty's absence of an hour and a half that Margaret Burns' remarkable recovery had been so fatally terminated.

That rough justice was being played out in the coroner's court is beyond doubt. At least one witness who came to the Exchange and who sat about waiting to give evidence was told to go home by Richard Statham, because it was unnecessary for her evidence to be taken. This was Martha Barton, the mother of Elizabeth Jones, Miss Burns' only intimate friend, who had recommended the use of the Welch's Female Powders and the Grains of Paradise, and who wanted to testify that Miss Burns had not been pregnant at all but had merely been suffering from the dropsy.

Tuesday the 29th of March was a black day for Angus. It was the second day of the inquest and he was at home in the morning when the Reverend John Vause called. The concerned clergyman had listened with interest to the part of the servants' evidence where it was stated that on the Friday morning Angus had not left the house at all. This struck him as odd, because he was convinced that on the Friday morning he had met Angus at the Athenaeum and walked home with him. Angus denied having been out on the Friday, telling Vause that it was the Thursday they had walked back from the Athenaeum. Vause, however, would have none of it.

How thorny this point was would become apparent when the prosecution outlined its theory. Simply put, the theory was this. If Miss Burns had borne a child on the Friday of her death, then Angus had got rid of it, and he had done so that morning on his way to the club.

Vause's place was taken by an even more unwelcome guest. The coroner had decided, without hearing much more evidence, that there was at the very least a strong case for taking Angus into custody, on suspicion of murder. For that purpose he despatched Constable Joseph Upton, one of the head constables of Liverpool, to Trinity Place with orders not only to arrest Angus, but to search the house from top to bottom for the body of a child and for any poisonous substance. It was not the first time Upton had been at Angus' house. He had also been there the previous day, according to his later testimony. What he had been doing there he didn't say. He certainly did not search for poison or a baby, or take away Miss Burns' clothes. One wonders if he would have been quite so inert if the enquiry had centred around some low house down by the docks. Angus was a respectable merchant, a man of considerable social standing, living in the most respectable district of the town, so it was probably more than Upton's job was worth to take it upon himself to turn the place upside down.

Now, on that Tuesday morning, Upton ordered Angus to hand over the keys to the house. Angus did not do so directly, but passed them to his brother-in-law who was present. Biggam and Constable Upton then went upstairs to Angus' bedroom, where Biggam unlocked the wardrobe which contained Angus' household medicines. What they found there, according to Upton, was a 'vast array of bottles' and a case of instruments - among the bottles were two marked, mysteriously, Jacob's Water, plus one marked Poison Water and another labelled Oleum Savin, or Oil of Savin. It was clearly the finding of the bottle marked Poison Water that stirred Constable Upton into making his arrest.

Angus was removed to the Borough Gaol in Water Street by Constable Upton, who later returned to the house and commenced his search. He found no sign of a baby but did not go away empty-handed. He was taken down into the cellar by Ann Hopkins, who handed over to him the clothes in which Miss Burns had died. Interestingly, the bedgown she had been wearing at the time was not among them. He passed the Poison Water bottle and the Jacob's Water bottles to Dr. Bostock for analysis, but not the Oil of Savin. This he showed at some stage to Steele the druggist, who confirmed that Angus had brought an identical bottle to him to be filled.

Angus remained in the Borough Gaol for the remainder of the inquest. The gaol, or the Tower as it was popularly known, was only a stone's throw from the church in which he had married Maria eight years before. How he must have reflected on his fortunes, or lack of them. The previous century it had been the place of confinement for several of the unfortunate followers of Bonnie Prince Charlie, many of whom had been tried and convicted under a special commission at Liverpool, and executed. When war with France broke out, it had filled up with naval prisoners of war. It was a grim, dirty and wretched place. The criminals were lodged in seven damp and miserable dungeons six and a half feet by five feet nine inches, and six feet high. These dungeons were ten steps underground, with an iron barred aperture above each cell door which admitted what light and air there was. As for health, that was totally disregarded. When the prison reformer John Howard had visited the gaol many years before, he had been appalled by the offensiveness and the overcrowding which had led to twenty-eight prisoners at one time being ill with gaol fever. Typhoid frequently carried off its inmates. Little had changed since his visit.

Fortunately for Angus there was a more airy dungeon which looked up onto the street through a grill. As it was not considered secure, generally only deserters were put into it. On Tuesday the 29th of March, Charles Angus became its newest occupant.

The prison allowance was a three-penny loaf of one pound three ounces to each prisoner daily, though for prisoners who could afford it and who had friends on the outside, it was possible to smuggle food in. Angus could certainly afford the one shilling per week which the gaoler required before he would supply a bed. In this miserable place, Angus had plenty of time to sit and ruminate on what was being said at the inquest, news of which was passed to him from the street.

One such bringer of news was another Liverpool physician, Dr. George Coltman, a fellow member of the Athenaeum, who had been visiting the prison to attend to the gaoler's wife. Coltman had been a surgeon's assistant in the navy, but had been dismissed from the service for striking his superior officer. He was a rough-spoken fellow, a political radical, and a profane swearer, whose bedside manner must have been something to behold. When Coltman remarked that Angus had once told him he was a light sleeper, and expressed surprise therefore at the fact that the servants had found it necessary to shake and jolt him, Angus for once had no explanation. 'I cannot say - I cannot account for it,' he answered.

Coltman would be called as a witness at the trial on account of this conversation, and for another reason besides. He had been standing on the steps of the Athenaeum one morning the previous week when he had shaken hands heartily with Angus. He would testify that to the best of his knowledge it was the Friday, the day that Angus denied ever leaving his house.

At the Exchange, the doctors finally gave their evidence, concluding that they were 'decidedly of the opinion that the deceased must have been delivered a short time before her death, of a foetus, which had arrived nearly at maturity'. It was not possible, they said, to account for the state in which they found the womb on any other supposition.

On the matter of poisoning, they were more guarded. It was 'highly probable', said their written report, 'that the uncommon change which the coats of the stomach had undergone had been occasioned by the introduction into the stomach of some unknown agent, capable of destroying the texture of that organ'. That 'unknown agent' would soon have a name to it, for Dr. Bostock had analysed the contents of the Poison Water bottle. He had found it contained corrosive sublimate of mercury, in which was saturated a strong solution of arsenic.

The jury, on the Friday evening, brought in a verdict of wilful murder against Charles Angus, and a few days later, on the 4th of April, Angus was committed to Lancaster Castle for trial at the next assizes. Lancaster Castle Gaol was at least better than the dreadful Borough Gaol, though it too had its dark and unwholesome cells which in summer were unbearably hot and suffocating. Felons and debtors were kept apart, the latter being allowed to work at spinning and knitting in the Crown and Shire Halls of the castle. Over the judge's bench in the latter was written the text 'Let Judgement run down as waters, and Righteousness as a mighty stream'.

Four days after Angus' arrival, the water of judgement carried a nineteen-year-old servant girl called Mary Chandley to the gallows at Lancaster Castle. She had been accused at the assizes just past of setting fire to her master's house in Liverpool to cover up a robbery, burning one of his children to death, and injuring another. Though she was found not guilty of the murder, she was nevertheless found guilty of the robbery, and sentenced to hang. She was described as being so ignorant of religious duties as to be unable to repeat the Lord's Prayer. As the executioner put the cap over her face, she exclaimed, 'Oh man, I will never forgive you!' Her shrieks were said to be extremely loud and piercing, and may well have reached Angus' ears.

That summer was a bleak one for Angus - himself in prison, one brother on his property in Jamaica up to no good and probably robbing him, another locked up in a private asylum having fits, his three children fatherless as well as motherless and without a governess to look after them. Luckily, his sister and brother-in-law, the Biggams, agreed to move into the house at Trinity Place and take care of seven-year-old Jane, five-year-old Maria, and four-year -old Thomas, for they had no children of their own. How supportive the Biggams were is impossible to know. Neither would give evidence at the trial, even though both had been on the scene within an hour of Miss Burns' death, and in spite of the fact that Mrs Biggam had sat up with Angus until the small hours of the following morning before finally taking herself home.

Elizabeth Biggam and her husband William, farmer's son turned cabinet maker, probably enjoyed having the occupancy of Angus' three-storey house, his furniture and his crockery. Whatever else Biggam was, he was in trade, and probably accustomed to putting in far more hours for less reward. Not for him the leisured life of the mercantile middle class, or the lucrative rewards (Angus' brother Alexander in only eight years in the port had amassed for himself a fortune worth twenty thousand pounds - it was only a pity he was locked up in the asylum and unable to enjoy it). Neither had Biggam enjoyed the luxury of marrying into money or property, even though Angus had graciously presented his wife with a wedding present of five hundred pounds. Of the Biggams, and their aspirations, we shall hear more later.

Now, however, it is time to make the acquaintance of the man whose name was soon to be linked to, and as notorious as Angus'. A fellow countryman whose career in the medical profession was to be blighted by his association with the case, and whose defence of Angus was to lead him to the social pillory.

It is time to meet Dr. James Carson.

❦ ❦ ❦

11   A Doctor's Dilemma

While Angus languished in Lancaster Gaol awaiting trial, three members of the Liverpool medical fraternity met one evening for dinner. The host was William Lucas Reay, a surgeon-apothecary who lived only a few doors from Trinity Place at 1, St. Anne Street. His guests were Thomas Fairfax Hay, who had accidentally enlarged the hole in Miss Burns' stomach with his fingers and who was also Reay's partner, and a thirty-six-year-old Scottish-born doctor called James Carson. Carson had an unusual background for a doctor, for he had originally trained as a Church of Scotland minister before deciding to take up medicine. This had provided him with an education in classical literature and philosophy which set him on a pedestal far above his two dinner companions.

After their hearty meal, the two surgeon-apothecaries asked Dr. Carson if he would care to inspect the stomach and uterus of Miss Burns. The offer of this additional delectation was gladly accepted, and Carson went with his companions to look at the organs which were preserved and floating in spirit. Carson, like half the medical fraternity in the town, was struck by the size of the uterus. He would also later say, however, that he doubted it had parted with a child, and that he made these doubts abundantly clear. This would be contested vehemently by Fairfax Hay who was aware of no doubts in Carson's mind.

Whatever the truth, it was the start of a controversy that was to reverberate around the port for many years to come.

Carson was no stranger to unorthodoxy or controversy. In fact he would spend the rest of his life courting it. He was a deeply frustrated man who longed for distinction, and who desperately sought the credit that had been showered upon many of his contemporaries. The loves of his life were literature and science, and it was the latter that he assiduously applied to the subject on which he had been fixed since his university days in Edinburgh - the circulation of the blood. It had almost been his undoing.

Long before that century it was known that the blood moved within the body, but it was envisaged that it did so in a to and fro motion from the heart. It took a pioneer of the seventeenth century, William Harvey, to discover that the blood did not just move but it circulated, and that it was the blood, impelled into the arteries, which gave rise to the pulse. Harvey's treatise on the subject was dedicated to Charles the First, and in it Harvey (perhaps wisely) compared the King to the heart, the centre of all strength and power. Though Harvey advanced no theory as to why the blood circulated, it was orthodox thinking by Dr. Carson's day that it was the power of the body alone which urged the blood to the completion of its circuit.

To Carson the young medical student this was not good enough. He was convinced that there had to be a more scientific reason why the blood went round the body. He went home and spent a sleepless night, turning the subject over and over in his mind.

Many great doctors and scientists have spent sleepless nights, and woken up to change the history of mankind. Dr. Carson was not one of them. The following morning he went to the residence of a friend and enthusiastically told him that he had discovered the causes of the motion of the blood. Put at its simplest, Carson's 'discovery' was that the pressure of the atmosphere played an important part, along with the resilience to that pressure of the lungs and arteries. Worse, Carson intended making his views the subject of an inaugural thesis. His friend, who later became a Professor of Chemistry at Glasgow, tried to talk him out of it, warning him that such doctrine would not be sufficiently orthodox for the college. He was proved right. Carson's thesis was, in the words of its writer, 'condemned in no measured terms by some of the most eminent members of the medical fraternity'.

Nevertheless, equipped with an Edinburgh degree, he moved to Liverpool where for the first few years he made a living by tending French naval prisoners of war. It was a lowly paid occupation. During his eight years in the town, Carson came up against his medical colleagues on many an occasion. It was hardly surprising therefore that he should start to rub them up the wrong way over the death of Miss Burns.

During that hot summer, experiments were going on in which dogs were given doses of corrosive sublimate of mercury, to see if the mercury could easily be found in their stomachs after death. On the 12th of July, Messrs Rutter, Gerard and Fairfax Hay gave a small dog forty drops containing about one and three quarter grains of sublimate, and a month later they repeated the experiment, giving a second dog two grains in solution on two separate occasions. In both cases the dogs died after much vomiting, and in both cases when they opened the stomachs Dr. Bostock could not find even the smallest trace of mercury. What this went to prove of course was nothing at all, except that the poison probably came up with the vomit, or Bostock's tests were not sophisticated enough to detect what remained. Nevertheless, from the jaws of failure, Bostock, Gerard, Rutter and Fairfax Hay would snatch victory. If dogs could be poisoned with mercury, and afterwards none of the poison be found, then so could Margaret Burns. It was on that simple equation that Angus' life hung by a thread.

One Sunday, Carson ran into Fairfax Hay at the Infirmary where the experiments were being conducted and asked if he could witness some of them. His reasoning appears devious. He wished to open the thorax of some animals as part of his continuing investigation into the motion of the blood. Examining the thorax would also have told him something else - how much corrosion and inflammation had taken place after the swallowing of the mercury. Fairfax Hay refused to let Carson anywhere near the experiments.

As the summer progressed, Carson began expressing his doubts to his own circle of friends. He was of the opinion that Miss Burns did not die of poison, that a hole in her stomach of any size could not be attributed to it, that she had not given birth. His ideas were so diametrically opposed to those of his colleagues that they came to the notice of Angus' solicitor, a young man of twenty-seven from Lancaster called Ephraim Atkinson. Carson sent the solicitor a letter setting out his opinions. On the question of the poisoning he was on safer ground than on the pregnancy. He could not explain how the uterus could be so enlarged, and the blood vessels distended, and the placenta so visible if a foetus had not been expelled. Atkinson was disappointed. There were cannons ranged against his client, and all he had was an empty gun. A defence theory had to be found, and fast.

He considered bringing up a doctor from London to testify. The practitioners in the capital were viewed as a different species of mortal who possessed a certain degree of infallibility. A London doctor would command a great deal of respect and ultimately increase Angus' chances of an acquittal. In the event, however, none could be found, even though right up until the evening of the trial it was strongly rumoured that a London anatomist had been found and would put in an appearance. It was all up to Dr. Carson.

The following day, Saturday, was a turning point in Carson's connection with the case. Although he had spent the weeks since his subpoena reading as much about the subject as he could, he still had no brilliant defence with which to ambush his colleagues. He had his own theories on what had caused the hole in Margaret Burns' stomach. It was the state of the uterus that was causing the problem. Ironically, the answer came from one of his patients, John McCulloch, who also happened to be a doctor.

McCulloch, another Scotsman, who had studied at Edinburgh, had been a surgeon aboard the Liverpool slave ships. At the end of one voyage, aboard the Bloom, he had received £8.4.4d in 'head money' for the number of slaves landed alive and well. Such satisfaction had he given that he was offered the command of his own vessel, but McCulloch preferred to return to Edinburgh where he finally qualified. He was a pillar of the Presbyterian Church in Liverpool, and - more importantly - had done a vast amount of obstetric work among the poor.

At that time, McCulloch was very ill, and Carson was tending not only McCulloch's patients but McCulloch himself. It was in the course of tending him for the last time before his departure for Lancaster that Carson got him talking about the case. McCulloch had no time for Carson's sentiments. McCulloch had seen the uterus, and firmly believed that it had parted with a child. He had also made up his mind that she had haemorrhaged to death - though how he had arrived at this conclusion is not clear. He had not been at the opening of the body, and had no direct knowledge of how much blood there had been, either in the room or on her clothes. In fact, the exact quantity of the blood was to be a frustratingly unresolved mystery at the trial.

Carson kept on. Weren't there many causes of distended wombs? Dropsies, tympanitic affections (swellings of gas in the belly)? Carson was back in his student days, searching for an answer that had eluded everybody, and which, like the muse, would settle on none other but James Carson. McCulloch racked his brains and came up with two patients of his who had suffered pains exactly resembling labour pains. Suddenly, Carson knew what his defence would be. If it wasn't sound, at least it was ingenious. To give an account now of what McCulloch told him would be to anticipate one of the major surprises of the trial. For the moment it is enough to say that Carson left McCulloch's bedside a happier man.

The assizes week was due to commence on Monday the 28th of August. At the eleventh hour, there was an event which caused a flurry of excitement in Liverpool. Ann Hopkins, the cook, was dragged before the coroner and charged with aiding and abetting Angus. Exactly why at this late stage Ann Hopkins should be sent for trial along with Angus says much about how desperate the parties for the prosecution were becoming. The official reason was that they had formed the belief that the birth of a child could not have taken place without the knowledge of the female servants, therefore one of them had to stand trial as well. The real explanation was probably very different. They needed at least one of the servants to give evidence that would convict Angus, and what better way than to charge one with being an accomplice and then encourage her to turn King's Evidence in return for freedom. This is exactly what Ann Hopkins was allowed to do.

About that time a poem appeared in Liverpool, printed in pamphlet form by G. Thompson of Church Street, and written by none other than William Roscoe, Liverpool's most famous citizen. William Roscoe, poet, writer, art collector, member of parliament, enemy of the slave trade, humanitarian, and founder of many Liverpool institutions including the Athenaeum, had written it primarily for his young son Robert. It was called 'The Butterflys' Ball and the Grasshoppers' Feast' and began with the lines :

> 'Come take up your hats, and away let us haste,
> To the Butterflys' Ball and the Grasshoppers' Feast,
> The Trumpeter, Gadfly, has summoned the crew,
> And the Revels are now only waiting for you'.

He might have penned it for the trial. As the inhabitants of the port took up their hats and hastened to Lancaster, the Revels were waiting for Charles Angus. The evidence would be flighty, to say the least.

12   Trial at Lancaster

'And there came the Beetle, so blind and so black,
Who carried the Emmett, his friend, on his back;
And there was the Gnat, and the Dragonfly too,
With all their relations, Green, Orange, and Blue'.
                                    'The Butterflys' Ball'

Across the Lancashire countryside they came, the travelling justices of the north, the hooves of their horses and the wheels of their post-chaises churning up the already appalling roads that led into Lancaster, the last assizes town of the circuit. Their dispensing of justice had taken them first to York, then onto Durham, Newcastle, Carlisle, Appleby, and finally on to the county town of Lancaster. They were accompanied by the barristers who knew nothing of what briefs they would be offered until they arrived, along with their servants, train bearers and porters. It was a hard, uncomfortable and uncertain life for all of them. Men made wills before travelling the roads that the itinerant justices of the Northern Circuit rode in those early days of the nineteenth century.

If it was hard for a judge, it was even harder for a junior barrister who might spend years on the circuit without ever getting a brief. The most important were snatched up and divided between senior counsel, and it was often a junior's lot to have to sit, watch and learn. Members of the bar were a rumbustious lot in those days. It was not uncommon for a judge to be flushed with claret, or for a barrister to get to his feet befuddled with drink and with precious few clues about what he was supposed to be talking about. Twenty-odd years before, James Boswell, the biographer of Dr. Johnson, had been a member of the Northern Circuit, and he had had his drunkenness disclosed in open court after attempting to use a Latin phrase the meaning of which totally eluded him and everybody else present. To gales of laughter, one of his colleagues interpreted the phrase *adhesit pavimento* as meaning 'stuck to the pavement, dead drunk' which is how Boswell had spent the previous night. The brief, as it turned out, was a cruel joke.

Lancaster was crammed to overflowing during assizes week. The judges arrived with their entourage on the Monday evening, and on the Tuesday morning, before proceeding to the castle, attended divine service at St. Mary's Church where they were treated to what the *Lancaster Gazette* called an 'excellent discourse' by the Reverend T. Moss, the Sheriff's Chaplain. Sermons were not short in those days, and often long on thunder and the Day of Judgement. Moss took his sermon from Deuteronomy. 'And what nation is there so great, that hath statutes and judgements so righteous as all this law which I set before you today?'

The judges then went into procession to the castle, and were blown in to court by the official trumpeters. Assizes had been held on this site since 1176. One of the most famous trials ever to take place there had been that of the Pendle Witches in the early seventeenth century, when ten inhabitants of that craggy hill country had been found guilty of witchcraft and executed. The court had been rebuilt since those dark and superstitious times, but still allowed sufficient room for the large crowds who attended the trials. At the back of the prisoner's dock was a branding iron, the red hot end of which was used to burn the letter M for malefactor on the brawn of the thumb of those convicted of felony. Across the court stretched the Judge's bench, above which, over the oak canopy, hung a life-size portrait of George the Third on horseback with the castle in the background, and towards the centre of the court was the jury box, so cramped that falling asleep was practically impossible. At the central table, the Clerk of the Court presided with the barristers and junior counsel. Courts in those days were almost public entertainments, so there was plenty of standing space for the frequently noisy mob. Justice was seen to be done, even if it was not always heard.

Before the trials proper began, there was the archaic procedure of presenting the evidence to a Grand Jury which was composed solely of local magistrates. This was not the same thing as the jury of twelve men who would decide on guilt or innocence. Their job was simply to weigh up the evidence, and decide whether each prisoner should be indicted or released. Angus had not been alone in the county gaol that summer. There were fifty-two other prisoners, whose crimes ranged from murder to bigamy, theft to the possession and uttering of forged notes. Those were the days of the industrial revolution, and many of the crimes were connected with the taking away and wrecking of machinery from mills and spinning works by those whose jobs were threatened. John Dobson, 46, was charged with 'breaking open a Fulling Mill and stealing a piece of woollen cloth, commonly called a Bocking Piece'. John Shaw, 24, was charged with stopping the spinning works of Messrs James Kay and Co., of Walmersley under the pretence of raising wages. John Hoyle, 34, of 'destroying tools and utensils used for weaving and preparing woollen cloth'. Six others were charged that they 'violently insulted Thomas Ashton of Heap to sign a Paper of Prices for the advance of wages to the weavers, and upon refusing, dragged him out into the highway and abused him'.

On a gentler note, there was John Torr, 27, who was accused of having three wives, and a young man called James Stott who had done little more than behave riotously by knocking on the door of the Reverend Thomas Drake of Castleton and shouting, 'His Majesty King George the Third is blind, thank God for it. I hope he will soon be no more - Damnation to all Royalists!'

The Grand Jury found True Bills against Angus and most of the accused. His trial opened at eight o'clock on the morning of Friday the 2nd of September. Angus was brought up from the cells, and up the steep steps to the trap door which opened into the prisoner's dock. *The Times* recorded the scene :

'The trial . . . attracted an immense concourse of people from all parts of the county; and the court, although capable of accommodating 1000 persons, was crowded at an early hour. At eight o'clock, the prisoner was placed at the bar. He is a tall, stout man and was dressed in black. The indictment charged him with having poisoned the deceased; and another count charged him with having given her poison to cause an abortion, she being pregnant'.

The judge, Sir Allan Chambre, was in his sixty-ninth year, and when he wasn't riding the circuit sat as one of the Justices of His Majesty's Court of Common Pleas, set up primarily to hear disputes between private individuals, at Westminster Hall. In his famous painting, Hogarth brilliantly caricatured the judges of the Common Pleas as a clutch of self-important bucolics slumbering beneath enormous periwigs. Fortunately Chambre had a high reputation at the bar both for his legal knowledge and the justice of his decisions. It was a Circuit custom that on Grand Night, a boisterous occasion, anyone publicly congratulated for anything at all should provide a gallon of wine for the mess. Chambre had been duly required to pay up when heartily congratulated for travelling the Circuit in a carriage decorated with a large cock.

As well as an amiable judge, among his defence team Angus had a rising star of an advocate. James Scarlet was neither a great lawyer nor an eloquent speaker, but he was on his way to being the finest barrister of his day. Handsome and gentlemanly, with a firmly modulated voice, he was also excessively vain. He never took notes of evidence, and never even prepared his speeches. His one object was to get a verdict by drawing on his own imperturbable self-possession. He had one thing in common with Angus - family connections in Jamaica. He had been born there, and was sent to England in the very same year that Angus, his heart full of adventure, had left Scotland for Liverpool. Though his family still held considerable property on the island, Scarlet had been brought up with a total abhorrence of the slave trade. His mother had separated him from it at an early age, keeping him away from slaves and all those who were in daily familiarity with them.

Scarlet, however, at this time was just one of two junior barristers, the other being Mr John Cross. The senior barrister for the defence was Mr James Topping, a member of the governing body of the Inner Temple.

Prosecuting counsel was Sergeant Cockell, a man with a bluff countenance and a hearty manner, who could put down witnesses with a

stroke and dramatise his case so powerfully that the most innocent frag-
ment would be shaded with guilt. The term Sergeant no longer exists in
law. It meant a senior practising barrister, having come from the French
sirviens, a common soldier or someone owing a special allegiance to the
King. It was Sergeant Cockell who would have the pleasure of opening
the case, and a hearty meal he would make of it too. He was assisted by
three juniors, Mr George Sawley Holroyd, Mr Jonathan Raine and Mr
James Clark.

The Clerk of Arraigns first read out the indictment, phrased in
the language of the day, which began, 'That Charles Angus late of
Liverpool in the County of Lancaster Merchant not having the fear of
God before his eyes but being moved and seduced by the instigation of
the Devil . . .'

Sergeant Cockell then opened the case for the prosecution, and
was hardly drawing his first breath when the words 'wilful murder, effect-
ed by means the most detestable, in the prosecution of the horrid dia-
bolical purpose' left his lips. He rightly said that the case had to be made
out by a train of circumstances, by Angus' own conduct previous to the
death of Miss Burns, by his conduct at the time - a clear reference to his
suspiciously deep slumber at a time when the body lay crumpled against
the wall - and to his not having told anybody for two days. Cockell went
on to outline Angus' Liverpool background, taking care to draw the
jury's attention to the fact he had once been an assistant to a druggist,
and then took them through the history of Miss Burns' painful illness.
When he arrived at the night of Thursday the 24th of March and the
morning of Friday the 25th, he left the jury in no doubt that in his opinion, during the hours of darkness, while the servants had been in bed and
Angus had been alone with Miss Burns in the parlour, the child had been
born.

He also laid the ground for the evidence that Ann Hopkins would
give, telling a rapt court that a large bandage or 'belly binder' had been
found about Miss Burns' person, that it was there to compress the body
after delivery and that she could not have tied it there herself. Like the
baby, it had since disappeared and could not be found.

He concluded with a reminder to the jury that if Angus had administered poison with a view to cause abortion, and without intending to kill the woman, it was still murder in the eye of the law. He then called his first witness, Betty Nickson the servant girl.

The court was in for its first surprise.

Betty told the court how she and the cook, Ann Hopkins, had only been in Angus' service for four weeks. Asked if she had any knowledge of Miss Burns before that time, she answered no. Her business was to make the beds and clean the rooms. During the time she had been there, Miss Burns had been in perfect health until the Wednesday morning of the 23rd of March. She did not know if Miss Burns had taken anything the day before that might have made her ill.

She recounted how she had seen Miss Burns come out of the parlour at six o'clock in the morning and go upstairs, and how, at about quarter to nine while breakfasting with Angus and the children she had seemed very ill indeed. Miss Burns remained in the parlour the whole day, while Angus was sometimes in one part of the house, sometimes in another. Then came an exchange the importance of which would soon become obvious.

Q : But was he out of the house at all that day, on the Wednesday?
A : No he was not.

It was vital for the prosecution to show that Angus had deliberately stayed in the house throughout Miss Burns' illness, since there was no way he could have known exactly when she would abort.

Holroyd then brought her round to Thursday the 24th when, she testified, Miss Burns vomited all day and evening. She took nothing but gruel, and declined a doctor. Angus, however, went out before dinner and stayed out until a little after three, when Betty let him in. This was his stated Thursday afternoon visit to his brother-in-law, Mr Biggam, in Brunswick Street. It was the first major obstacle for the prosecution. If Angus was poisoning Miss Burns with a view to causing a miscarriage, why had he not stayed by her side? Why had he left her in the care of the two servants?

On the Thursday night, Betty testified, both she and the cook went in and offered to sit up with Miss Burns, but Angus declined their offer, giving as his reason the fact that he couldn't sleep because of the worry over his brother Alexander.

She described how, on the morning of Friday the 25th - the fatal day - she had been rung for at four o'clock to attend to the children who were crying in the nursery, and to fetch a jug of cold water for Angus. Miss Burns, she said, appeared to be much worse and her breathing quicker. This was crucial testimony. It if was true, it almost certainly meant that at four o'clock on the Friday morning the baby had not yet been born. Betty went back to bed, and at six o'clock came downstairs again, this time with Ann Hopkins. Only two hours had elapsed. In those two hours, Miss Burns had suddenly become well enough to want some warm beer. Had the baby therefore been born, or had the miscarriage taken place, between the hours of four and six on that Friday morning? This was what the court was being invited to believe.

Betty told the court of how Angus, wearing his flannel morning dress, gave her a note at ten o'clock that morning to go to Mr Winstanley's, the wine merchant of Henry Street, nearly half a mile away. In actual fact, Henry Street was three quarters of a mile from Trinity Place as the crow flies. Because of her sprained foot she was absent roughly an hour and ten minutes. She had returned with the wine shortly after eleven and gone straight into the parlour. She was shocked to find Miss Burns 'cowered of a lump, with her elbows upon her knees, and her face against the wall'.

Q : Did you observe your master when you went in?
A : Not at first, sir - I did not go in, but saw her just at thedoor, and ran back into the kitchen.
Q : What did you do after that?
A : I went to the cook in the kitchen.
Q : What did you and the cook do then?

A : I asked her where mistress was, for I could not believe it was her at first.

Who had Betty believed the cowered figure against the wall was? She described the waking of Angus, how the cook laid her on the sofa, while she went for Mrs Biggam, Angus' sister. She then recounted the removing of the clothes, and the laying out of the body upstairs. No medical person was sent for, she told the court, from the Friday morning when Miss Burns died until the Sunday morning. Angus, however, at some period over the weekend - Betty seemed a little vague as to when it was - spent two hours in the parlour with her and Ann Hopkins, talking of Miss Burns' goodness to him and the children.

Betty was then asked about Angus' children.

Q : You were about the children a good deal, were you?
A : Yes.
Q : Of course then you must know whether their ears were bored?
A : No - they were not bored.
Q : You are sure of that?
A : Yes.

This effectively made Angus' assertion that he wanted his 'instrument' sharpened so that he could bore his children's ears look like a blatant lie.

Betty's examination was over. The doctors lined up for the prosecution would comment afterwards that her account of Miss Burns' symptoms had been much more full and particular at the inquest. There was, for instance, no mention of her extreme thirst or of her having to grip the sides of the sofa. Mr Topping, for the defence, was hardly on his feet when, under cross-examination, Betty contradicted herself. She was being asked about Angus' movements on the Wednesday morning when Miss Burns had first been taken ill. Topping reminded her that at six o'clock she had seen Miss Burns leave the parlour and go upstairs.

Q : At that time your master was in bed, I believe; he had not
come downstairs, had he?

A : Yes, he had gone out to read the news.

JUDGE : It was six o'clock, you said, when you first
saw Miss Burns - your master had not gone
out then?

A : Yes, he had.

TOPPING: He was in the habit, was he not, of going
out in the morning to read the news?

A : Yes, he used to go out when it was fine.

This was completely new. In her first examination, Betty had told
the court that Angus had not left the house on the Wednesday. Now she
was saying that he had. What was even more remarkable was that,
according to one Athenaeum member who would give evidence, the
newsroom did not open until seven o'clock. What was Angus doing out
of the house at six - if indeed he was?

Topping extracted from her the important fact that Miss Burns, as
housekeeper, had the keys of the doors and cupboards, including the
wardrobe in Angus' bedroom where he kept his medicines. The possibility that Miss Burns had taken something herself during this time to end
her pregnancy had to be planted firmly in the minds of the jury.

Mr Raine's re-examination for the prosecution was extremely
short, but it contained the most dramatic revelation. Raine first of all
seized on Betty's evidence that Angus had gone out of the house by six
o'clock on the Wednesday morning.

Q : Now are you sure that it was a quarter before six that your
master went out to read the news? (He was putting it even
earlier).

A : Yes it was.

Suddenly, Angus threw his own question from the dock. He

demanded that she tell the court whether or not he had gone out at all on the Friday, the day of Miss Burns' death. Betty stared across the crowded courtroom at him and answered, like a dutiful servant, 'No, you were not, sir'.

Then came the bombshell. Mr Raine asked the judge to put a completely new question to the witness.

RAINE : Will your Lordship have the goodness to ask whether on the Friday morning, at an early hour, she went to Everton with the children?

JUDGE : Did you go out to Everton with the children on the Friday morning?

BETTY : Not with the children.

JUDGE : Did you go without the children?

BETTY : Yes, about seven o'clock.

JUDGE : How long might you be absent?

BETTY : About half an hour.

JUDGE : Are you quite sure that this was on the Friday morning?

BETTY : Quite so, indeed.

RAINE : Whether it was her practice or habit, My Lord, to do so.

JUDGE : Were you in the habit of going to Everton early in the morning?

BETTY : Yes, every morning while I lived there.

JUDGE : Did you go there only to take the children in general?

BETTY : We went for milk and cream.

The more astute members of the jury would have detected something very sinister in this. Betty Nickson had said nothing about going to fetch the milk and cream from Everton in her previous examinations. Her only expedition on the morning of Miss Burns' death had been much later, to fetch wine from Mr Winstanley's, a journey that had taken her by contrast an hour and ten minutes. Of course, it may have been that the journey to Everton was so much part of her daily routine that she forgot to mention it - and to be fair, she was never asked. What was so puzzling about this journey to Everton was that she had not taken the children with her.

Counsel cannot cross-examine their own witnesses, and so the mystery was never cleared up. There must have been those however who asked themselves if Betty Nickson did not go to Everton with another purpose, a purpose that would make the taking of the children impossible.

Did she have a bundle under her arm containing a dead baby, and did she dispose of it somewhere in the open countryside, possibly by burying it?

If anything, this evidence suggested that Betty Nickson, not Ann Hopkins, should have been charged with aiding and abetting.

Ann Hopkins' evidence was less dramatic and even less revealing. She began her evidence grudgingly, prepared to give little more than that Miss Burns complained slightly and felt poorly on the Wednesday that she fell ill. It was clear from the outset that she, too, was going to be a difficult prosecution witness. She obviously felt that her immunity from prosecution, once guaranteed, meant that she could turn King's Evidence back on itself. And this she did. Her testimony was striking for one reason only. Ann Hopkins knew nothing.

On the Wednesday evening, she said, she wanted to know if they should make a fire in the governess' bedroom, and bring their beds down bedside hers, but the offer was declined. It was Miss Burns, she stressed, who refused the offer - not Angus.

Q : Did you observe, just before you went to bed, how Miss Burns was?

A : She seemed very poorly, I did not take notice, not how she was, she seemed very poorly when we went to bed, on Wednesday night.

Q : Did she complain at all, at that time?

A : Not to me, sir, she did not.

And that was all she would be drawn on. Ann Hopkins' evidence about the Thursday concerned the making of the water posset with buttermilk, which she stated she did not see Miss Burns drink, and the beer which she said Betty Nickson heated and gave to the governess. She did say however that the vomit was of a blacker colour than on the Wednesday. Miss Burns had also been bothered by retention of urine, which Ann Hopkins claimed had been alleviated by the sliced onion she had given her to sit on. This pearl of domestic wisdom effectively ended Ann Hopkins' involvement with Miss Burns on the Thursday. The cook said she did not even go in that night to see how Miss Burns was, but went straight to bed. (Betty Nickson had testified they both went in that night and offered once again to sit up with Miss Burns).

Giving evidence about the Friday, she intimated that she got up a little later than usual, 'between six and seven, rather after six that morning'. A bell was rung before she went into the parlour, about ten minutes later. Angus was sitting in his easychair, Miss Burns was lying on the sofa, and she seemed to have made a miraculous recovery for she was saying the pain had left her and asking for warm beer. As well as the warm beer, Miss Burns had about a pint of gruel. Then, between ten and eleven, after Betty Nickson had been sent to the other side of Liverpool for the wine, Angus and Miss Burns ordered dinner, along with some barley water. Ann Hopkins left the parlour and went downstairs to the kitchen to prepare it.

If Ann Hopkins' evidence was true, then only one person in the court knew what happened in the parlour in that half hour before Betty returned. That person was standing in the dock.

Betty Nickson's return and the waking of Angus was described by Ann Hopkins.

Q : Who first went up to him?
A : I did.
Q : Did you speak?

A : I did not speak, but shook him first.

Q : Did Betty speak?

A : She screamed.

Q : When Betty screamed, was he awake then?

A : Not seemingly, he was not.

Q : Then you shook him?

A : I shook him, sir.

Q : How long did you shake him before he awoke?

A : I seemingly shook him a good bit before he awoke.

Q : When he awoke, what did he say?

A : He stood, and said, my God! He said - what is this. Sir, said I, Miss Burns is dead. Dead! he says, dead! and I said, Yes.

This was probably the most lucid and descriptive piece of Ann Hopkins' testimony. She would soon lapse back into her grudging self. She described how, after the arrival of the Biggams and Elizabeth Jones, Mrs Biggam, Elizabeth Jones and herself, along with Betty Nickson, carried the body upstairs. From the body she took a flannel gown, a flannel petticoat, a shift and a pair of stockings.

She also admitted to removing two cloths that were round her thighs, held by a piece of tape. She would not be drawn on the existence of any bandage around the waist used as a 'belly binder' after delivery.

The cook was not out of the pot yet. James Scarlet rose to cross-examine. He established she had not known Angus or Miss Burns before she went to work at Trinity Place. Then he asked her the ages of Angus' children. It had nothing to do with the case, but at least it signalled to the jury that were they to send Angus to the gallows, three very young children would be left parentless in the world. Jane, she said, was seven, Maria five, and Thomas a little more than three. (Maria had actually turned six and Thomas four while their father had been in gaol).

Under the gentlest of cross-examinations, she affirmed that on the Wednesday Angus definitely went out at seven o'clock - not six o'clock - to read the papers. The rest of her evidence, however, was notable for what she could not speak about. From eleven o'clock on the Thursday morning, she said, until she got up on the Friday - a period of almost nineteen hours - she did not go into the parlour at all. She knew nothing about the vital period leading up to the time when the baby was either born or aborted. In other words, about what she did not know she could not testify.

This was a boon to the defence, and wisely Scarlet left it at that. He did not even remind her that her fellow servant had given evidence regarding them both going in on the Thursday evening. He scored another point by getting her to admit that the cloths around Miss Burns' thighs may have been there 'because she was in a certain situation', a coy way of implying that Miss Burns may actually have been menstruating!

What had Ann Hopkins been doing for those nineteen hours? The matter remained unresolved. More to the point, she was not asked and did not say whether Angus had left the house on the all-important Friday morning.

The next witness was Angus' next-door neighbour, Sarah Lawson. She had little to add except that three or four weeks before her death, Miss Burns appeared to be in a state of pregnancy. She had seen her pass the window on two occasions in the week before she died, and her opinion had only been strengthened. Asked how Miss Burns' health appeared to be on the Tuesday, the day before she fell ill, Sarah Lawson replied that 'she appeared to be in perfect health' adding, cryptically, 'at least I thought so'.

The two witnesses who followed advanced the prosecution case little. Mary Clark, who kept the public house round the corner, said that she had served Miss Burns with ale twice a day and that about Christmas she 'perceived her to grow larger'. The last time she saw her was a week or ten days before her death, and she appeared then to be a great deal larger. Mary Clark, who had borne nine children herself, was in no doubt that Miss Burns was pregnant. Such was also the observation of her sister, Alice Tellett, who lived with her. Under cross-examination, both women confessed that they had no intimacy or acquaintance with her other than as a neighbour.

The evidence of Betty Nickson's mother, Jane Nickson, was more damaging. She told the court that she had given birth to twelve children, not all of whom had survived, and that she had seen Miss Burns twice on visits to her daughter at Angus' house. She was asked if Miss Burns had the appearance of a pregnant woman. 'Yes sir, if ever I had,' she replied.

On the day of Miss Burns' death, she had visited the house and thought to herself what a state she had died in. She spoke about the laying of salt on the corpse, to which she gave, perhaps unintentionally, a sinister interpretation - it was to take the swelling down, she said. Cross-examined, she agreed that she had placed salt on the corpses of her own children, and that it was no uncommon thing.

Mary Peat then took the witness box and transported the jury back to that moonlit night a year ago when, disturbed by a dream, she had gone to the nursery in which Miss Burns slept, only to find her not in the children's bed.

> JUDGE : For anything you know to the contrary, she might
> be sitting below in the parlour?
> A : Yes sir.

She continued with her tale of how she had made the bed two or three mornings, and found no crease in it, no mark of a person having lain there. It was 'high up' whereas the part where the children lay was 'pressed down'. She also narrated the story of the candlestick, which Miss Burns generally took to bed with her, and which one morning she had found on Angus' bedroom table along with the tinderbox.

Topping, for the defence, sought to establish that there was nothing secret about Miss Burns going into Angus' bedroom in the morning, and that for all she knew Angus might have taken the candlestick and tinderbox for some purpose of his own. As for the bed, Miss Burns used to assist Mary Peat in making the beds, and the servant agreed that Miss Burns might already have made up the children's bed before she (Mary) went into the room. More importantly, Topping drew from her the fact that there was no place in the bed which separated Miss Burns and the children, and so if her observations were true, it meant that young Jane and Maria had stayed on their side of the bed all night.

As with the servants, the candlestick and the tinderbox had shed little light on the mystery.

Into the witness box stepped the lecherous Liverpool clergyman, John Vause. He told how it was on the Friday morning that he had met Angus at the Athenaeum and walked home with him. It could not have been on the preceding day as he had been unwell. He was as equally certain it could not have been on the Monday, the Tuesday or the Wednesday.

Regarding his conversation with Angus after the death of Miss Burns, Vause said that he himself suggested Miss Burns might have been 'quacking' herself, as he knew Angus kept a medicine chest in the house.

> VAUSE : I asked him if he himself had given her any, and his reply was 'she had a black puke; seven drops of laudanum one night, and ten drops of laudanum another'.
>
> Q : Can you recollect the very expression he used about the black puke?
>
> VAUSE : The words were that she had a black puke and seven drops of laudanum one night, and ten drops another.

This nonsense was followed by an account of Angus' assertion that the governess had died of a fit, possibly brought on by a vaginal discharge, and a bizarre explanation Angus had supposedly given him for her increased size, that it was caused by the way she had plaited her flannel petticoat over her waist.

The black puke would not stay down. Angus had made it clear to Vause on the clergyman's second visit that what he had meant by the black puke was vomit, that it was not something he had given her. Vause attempted to correct the earlier impression he had given. He said that Angus had admitted giving Miss Burns some tartar emetic during the preceding week when she had complained of being ill.

'His answer was, he meant to say not that the puke he had given her was black, but that the contents of the stomach which she had thrown up, which were either first black and then green, or first green and then black, I don't exactly recollect - and added, that he had given her that morning some castor oil in some spirit, which had come up immediately.'

The judge was becoming exasperated. Yet out of this muddle had come something new. The jury had not heard from either servant about Miss Burns being given castor oil by Angus.

The castor oil was vitally important. The prosecution were well aware that in a case of poisoning they had to prove that the defendant had both possession of poison and the opportunity to administer it. Had the poison therefore been in the castor oil which, as every child knew, had a most disgusting taste and might disguise something equally unpleasant?

Q : What was the expression he used?

A : That he 'had given her some castor oil that morning' - so I understand. I will not be positive as to his saying 'that morning' but he certainly said he had given her some castor oil in spirit which had come up.

Q : Can you say that he positively mentioned when he had given her that? : To the best of my recollection, it was that morning (the morning of her death).

Q : And it came up immediately?

A : It came up immediately.

James Scarlet rose to cross-examine. He could not shift Vause on the matter of Angus being out on the Friday morning. Vause was encouraged however to say that he perceived nothing different in Angus' manner, conversation or appearance. Vause even went along happily with Scarlet's suggestion that Angus' 'agitation of mind', brought on by his brother's derangement of intellect might have led to him going to the Athenaeum on that Friday morning and not being able to remember it.

Scarlet had skilfully had it both ways. Angus had been composed and quite his normal self, and yet he had been so agitated that he couldn't remember what he had done.

Vause's cross-examination ended with the clergyman denying that he had ever gone to Angus' house out of idle curiosity. His duty, as he saw it, was to rescue Angus from 'a foul imputation'. Scarlet congratulated him. 'Well sir, I have no doubt that such were your motives.'

The prosecution could not leave it at this. They had the right to re-examine and used it. Holroyd was soon on his feet, and attempted to bring up the black puke for the umpteenth time. This was too much for the judge. Sir Allan Chambre's patience with the black puke finally cracked. He snapped, 'You have made so much confusion between the black puke, the emetic, and the tartar, that I declare it is almost unintelligible'. He was probably speaking for many in the court.

After Vause came Dr. George Coltman, the rough spoken physician. Coltman was also asked about seeing Angus at the Athenaeum. Fixing the day from an event which happened the day after, he said that it was on the Friday, a few minutes before seven o'clock, that Angus had shaken his hand very heartily on the newsroom steps. The jury had it from two witnesses. Holroyd was anxious to ascertain when the newsroom opened, to lay to rest once and for all Betty Nickson's assertion that Angus had been out of the house before six o'clock on the morning Miss Burns fell ill. Coltman told the court that the newsroom regularly opened at seven in the morning, and as regularly closed at ten in the evening. Coltman himself had been one of the first proprietors of the newsroom. Asked if it ever opened a little before six, Coltman was adamant it did not.

'No, sir, never - I myself have been on the committee, and have always strenuously endeavoured to defend the rights and privileges of the Master of the Coffee Room.'

This glorious answer, which illuminated the minor workings of Liverpool's most treasured institution, ended Coltman's examination. He was not cross-examined.

James Cheyne the insurance broker followed. Cheyne added little, other than his own observations of Miss Burns' size while he was once dining at Angus' house, and his opinion that she was 'with-child'. He could not say how far pregnant she might have been. The jury got its first indication that Angus was at least ambivalent on the matter of abortion. This was the mysterious 'lady from Liverpool' who had gone to the Isle of Man. While Angus had said that the man who was guilty of such a thing had acted very improperly, he 'supposed it was possible to have given her something to carry it off'.

The portrait painter Jeremiah Steele told the court how around Christmas Angus had pointed to a naked female in a book on anatomy at Dr. Traill's, and said that if he touched a certain part of the mouth of the womb, it would cause an abortion. For the defence, Mr Topping sought to instantly limit the damage done by this evidence.

> Q : This, I suppose, was a sort of subject which you, as a
>   portrait painter, know nothing about?
> A : Certainly.
> Q : Men who turn their minds to medical purposes don't con-
>   sider it a great secret?
> A : Dr. Traill expressed himself so.
> Q : Now though Mr Angus mentioned this, he condemned the
>   use of it, did he not, saying he had taught it one of the young
>   men whom he had sent on board an African ship, and he
>   believed he had made an improper use of it?
> A : Yes.

Jeremiah Steele's place in the witness box was taken by Henry Glover Moore, who purported to have witnessed much more than Miss Burns' increased size. He recounted his moonlit investigation of the open sash window that looked into Angus' parlour, and how he had seen Angus and Miss Burns sitting close together, kissing. This earned a rebuke from the judge.

> MOORE : Their faces were to each other - I was not so near as

to see whether they absolutely touched, but I have
no doubt in my own mind, he was giving her a kiss.

JUDGE : You are to tell us what you saw, and what you can
speak to positively, not what you have any doubt
about. Were their faces close together?

MOORE : I cannot speak to that, my Lord.

It is hard to see how Glover Moore could have witnessed Angus giving Miss Burns a kiss if their faces had not been close together. What is also curious is that Glover Moore timed this event to the August of the previous year. That neatly left a gap of eight months before Miss Burns died, 'delivered of an almost fully grown child'. One wonders if it was not altogether too calculated.

The Reverend James Gildart was the second clergyman to give evidence, which was, mercifully, free of black pukes. He merely told the court of his conversation with Angus about concealed marriages being unsafe because they might produce fruits, and Angus' reply that such effects could be prevented.

Peter Charnley the retired timber merchant now blew in from Angus' past. Twelve or thirteen years had elapsed since the day that Angus had shown him a silver tube-like instrument with a slide that ran up the centre and a three edged dart at the point. Charnley explained to Sergeant Cockell how Angus told him that by introducing it into the womb, and letting the air in, a miscarriage could be brought about. Asked if he could now recognise it if he saw anything like it, he replied that he might.

An instrument was then handed to him to look at. The jury, to a man, stared at it. Was this the evil object? Charnley said it looked something like the one, but after such a long period of time he could not be sure. Sergeant Cockell then asked him an equally pointed question.

'Now, sir, it is my duty, and I assure you it is far from being a pleasant one, to ask you whether any mention was made about any connection of his own?'

Charnley said he didn't particularly recollect. Sergeant Cockell said he wouldn't press him. Had Angus sown a few wild oats in his care-free bachelor days, and needed to resort to such methods? The court was kept in the dark about this.

Thomas Richardson, the cutler and surgeons' instrument maker, next took the stand. He told how Angus had brought the instrument to his shop to have it sharpened 'uncommon keen' and that its purpose was for boring his childrens' ears. (The jury now knew from Betty Nickson's evidence that none of Angus' children had pierced ears). He was handed the instrument and said that it was not the one, though it was exactly like it.

No evidence would be adduced of any such instrument being found at Trinity Place. One can only surmise that the prosecution had procured something identical. Such instruments were not uncommon.

Q : Is it a fit instrument for that purpose?
A : Not at all, it would rather abuse the ear than otherwise.
Q : Do you make instruments for the purpose of boring ears?
A : I have made several.

Richardson was handed another instrument with which to compare the one already in his hands. He said that the second one was exactly for that purpose.

Q : Now what is the difference between the points of the two?
A : The one nearly resembles a stocking needle, and the other has a triangular point.
Q : And that would hurt the ear?
A : It would make a hacking wound.

The various strands which made up the web of circumstantial evidence were gossamer thin, but they were growing. More strands were added to that web by the evidence of John Steele, the druggist, who told the court that about six weeks before Miss Burns' death he had sold Angus the quarter ounce of Oil of Savin. Angus had originally wanted an

ounce, but was not prepared to pay five shillings for it. Steele had put the
Oil of Savin into a phial which Angus had brought with him.

Q : Now what is Oil of Savin - is it poisonous?

A : I always considered it as such.

Q : Do you know whether it will cause abortion?

A : I do not, except from information; I have heard so, but
I do not know it for a certainty.

Q : Is it your practice to sell it to women?

A : No sir. We are suspicious they may make an improper use of
it.

Steele also said he did not sell it to men who were strangers to
him, but that as Angus was no stranger, he sold it freely. When Constable
Upton had shown him a phial taken from Angus' wardrobe which had
Oleum Sabine upon the cork, he had identified it as the one Angus had
brought in to be filled. It no longer contained Oil of Savin but another
oil called Pennyroyal, also an abortifacient.

At last Constable Upton took the witness box. Here was the man
who had searched the house for the body of a child, taken possession of
the bottles and of Miss Burns' clothes, and delivered Angus into custody.
Unfortunately, Constable Upton was no Georgian Sherlock Holmes.
Poisoning cases were quite outside his sphere of duty or experience.

Q : Did you make a very minute search for the body of the child?

A : I did.

Q : Did you succeed in the object of your search?

A : No. I was not able to find it.

And that was all he had to say on the matter. How minute
Constable Upton's search was we shall never know. Considering the possibility that Angus may have disposed of the body on the way to the
Athenaeum on the Friday morning, it may have been equally fruitful to
have conducted a search of the streets between Trinity Place and Church

Street, and the open land immediately to the east. If any such search was carried out, it was not mentioned.

Upton listed the clothes which Ann Hopkins had given him from the cellar. They comprised a shift, a flannel petticoat, a pair of womens' cotton stockings, a pair of bandages tied together at each end (the two cloths) and a 'piece of flannel' (probably the waistcoat). Attentive members of the jury would now be aware that one item was missing - the flannel bedgown that Miss Burns had been wearing when she died, and which Ann Hopkins said she had taken down into the cellar also. If Ann Hopkins did give it to Constable Upton, what happened to it? Was it also covered in blood?

Upton was requested to produce the clothes, and brought out a box. The clothes spilled out in a bundle. He held them up one by one, as well as the piece of tape which had held the two bandages or cloths together. He said they had been very wet and bloody at the time. He was clearly uncomfortable showing them to the jury for Sergeant Cockell, on the judge's suggestion, told him to put them away. And so Margaret Burns' clothes were returned to the box and nothing more was said about them. Possibly too much time spent dwelling on a dead woman's undergarments was seen as distasteful in a courtroom more accustomed to loom wreckers and possessors of forged notes.

It was time for the doctors to have their say. With Thomas Fairfax Hay's entrance into the witness box, the prosecution reached its final stage.

He began by describing the post mortem carried out on the body of Miss Burns, admitting that with his own fingers he accidentally enlarged the hole in the lower part of the stomach. He could not account for it other than by some 'deleterious drug', adding that independent of that organ he had never examined a more healthy or a fresher subject. Turning to the uterus, he said it was a healthy uterus the size of a bullock's heart, with evident marks of recent attachment by a placenta. In his opinion, the child must have been fully grown.

Asked to describe in more detail the appearance of the uterus, he told the court that the general cavity was smooth, the part where the placenta had been attached was rugged, and that the vessels going from the uterus to the placenta mark for the nourishment of the child were plainly discernible. He also stated that the peritoneal coat on the upper part of the uterus was slightly inflamed - a fact which had not been included in their report to the coroner.

Cross-examining, Scarlet suggested that a considerable change might have taken place in the internal organs following Miss Burns' death. Fairfax Hay answered that there was very little evidence of putrefaction. Scarlet's next question involved experiments that other medical authorities had recently carried out to prove that the stomach could be 'digested' after death by nothing more sinister than the action of the gastric juices. Was Fairfax Hay acquainted with the writings of Mr John Hunter on that subject? The humble surgeon and anatomist said that he was. John Hunter was a renowned surgeon and anatomist who had died fifteen years before, and who is now regarded as the father of modern surgery. Fairfax Hay responded by saying that the stomach was not in a state of digestion, it was in a destroyed state. The hole was not what he would call digestion, but a destruction. Hunter's opinions were no more than speculation, he added.

He agreed that holes had been found in stomachs after death that could not be accounted for by natural causes, and where there was no suspicion of poison, but this according to Fairfax Hay's reading and experience only happened in healthy stomachs which showed no previous disease. This answer must have delighted Angus' defence. Only a few moments before he had implied that independent of the effects in the stomach he had never examined a more healthy subject. Scarlet was not ready to let him off the hook. 'Are you acquainted with the book of Morgagni?' he asked.

A : I have never read it.

Q : You have never read Morgagni's book, *De Sebidus et Causis Morborum?*

A : No, sir.

It is extremely doubtful that James Scarlet had read it either. But the point was made. The greatest work, running to five volumes, of Giovanni Battista Morgagni, the founder of pathological anatomy and the discoverer of cirrhosis of the liver and many forms of tumour, had never been read by Fairfax Hay.

Scarlet forced Fairfax Hay to agree that the action of such a deleterious drug must have been very violent. If so, he asked, would not such a drug have produced apparent effects of violence upon other parts? Fairfax Hay declined to answer, advising that Dr. Bostock was the proper person to enlighten the court on that matter.

Dr. Gerard then took up the torch for the prosecution. His qualifications were far more impeccable. He said he had been in general practice as an accoucheur for about five or six years, and had attended at least five hundred cases of childbirth. He had also been a physician for twenty-four years. In his opinion, the preternatural opening in the stomach was the cause of death. He could not attribute it to any known disease, to any act of external violence, to any excess vomiting, or to putrefaction. He had contemplated corrosion by the gastric juice, but the appearances differed from those described by Hunter. Furthermore, Gerard said, other celebrated authors had failed to observe the phenomenon. He cited another Italian author, Spallanzani, who had made experiments purposefully after reading of Hunter's findings and had failed to observe a hole through the coats of the stomach.

Nobody was going to accuse Dr. Gerard of not reading up on his subject.

Asked about the effects of Oil of Savin on the human body, Gerard could only describe the effects it had had on a dog. Though the animal had died, and slight corrosion of the internal coat of the stomach had been found, there was no hole right through by any means. Gerard was not of the opinion that Oil of Savin had caused the death of Miss Burns. He was of the opinion however that corrosive sublimate of mercury taken in solution 'might be capable of producing deleterious effects, and not afterwards be discovered in the stomach, which has since proved to be a fact'.

It was a fact that no corrosive sublimate of mercury had been found in Miss Burns' stomach. Like Fairfax Hay before him, Dr. Gerard was going to leave the difficult part to Dr. Bostock.

Moving on to the womb, Gerard said that the child must have been so near full term that it might have lived, had it been born alive. He was as perfectly satisfied that a child had been expelled from the womb as he would have been if he had seen it with his own eyes. He agreed that vomiting, thirst and pain frequently attended labour as well as poison, but that where both existed these symptoms would be increased considerably. He took two opportunities to hammer home the point that Angus' servants had failed to describe the symptoms Miss Burns had suffered from as fully and as strongly as they had at the inquest, a fact which clearly frustrated him.

The cross-examination by Mr Cross, junior counsel for the defence, was for its time a textbook example of how to make an expert witness look much less so in the witness box. Firstly he drew the admission that having found what they supposed an adequate reason for her having died, the perforation, they subsequently neglected to examine any other organ. Gerard was immediately put on the defence. Nevertheless, Cross stressed, the head had not been opened, or the thorax. Gerard had to concede that was the case.

Gerard told the court that he had examined about twenty stomachs as critically as he had examined this one, and had not found a hole in any of them. It was not from his own knowledge then, Cross presumed, that such a hole was a preternatural thing? Gerard's reply was hopelessly confused.

'I conceive it to be a preternatural thing from my own knowledge, because it is only described to happen in a natural state as the effect of the gastric juice - if you mean a natural state from the action of the gastric juice, it may arise from that action after death, but not as a natural state, any further than as the effect of the gastric juice'.

To Cross' ingenious suggestion that an ulcerated area might have been more susceptible, Dr. Gerard would not venture to give an opinion. Pressed to give one, he said he believed ulceration was capable of leading to the forming of a hole, but that the previous symptoms would have been of much longer duration than just three days.

The final witness for the prosecution was Dr. Bostock. So much now hinged on his evidence. Though he had not been present at the opening of the body, he had seen the stomach and believed the hole to be produced by some 'poisonous substance taken into it'. He had no experience of corrosive sublimate of mercury taken in solution, but was of the opinion that such poison would produce such an effect. It was, he explained, a substance frequently used in medicine, but if taken in sufficient quantity it was a very active poison. Then came the most categoric reply of any of the medical witnesses. Asked if it was not possible that, after a person had taken such a poison, and been affected with vomiting and purging, and also taken a large quantity of fluid into the stomach, no trace of poison might be found, Bostock stated,

'That question I am able to answer in the affirmative most decisively. Corrosive sublimate may be taken into the stomach in a state of solution, and death may take place after violent symptoms of vomiting, purging, and drinking copiously of diluted liquors, but on examination of the stomach and its contents after death, the most minute examination will not be able to discover, or detect, any of the corrosive sublimate of mercury'.

Dr. Bostock was saying that because poison could not be found, it was undetectable.

Bostock testified that he had examined the uterus and found it large enough to contain a quart of fluid, whereas an unimpregnated uterus had scarcely any cavity. In that state, it was 'scarcely larger than a pear or a fig'. From the appearance of the part to which the afterbirth had been attached, and the dilatation of the mouth of the womb, he was inclined to say that the extracted foetus must have been considerably advanced. He was the third witness to be in no doubt about this.

Referring to the bottles he had received from Constable Upton, he said that the bottle marked Poison Water contained a considerable quantity of arsenic. He was prepared to speak with almost equal certainty to it containing corrosive sublimate - again a considerable quantity.

The fluid contained, he said, as much of the arsenic and corrosive sublimate as it would dissolve, that indeed it was saturated with those substances.

Curiously, Bostock was not asked, and did not volunteer any information about the contents of the other two bottles marked Jacob's Water. We can only conclude that whatever was in them had proved to be innocuous. Even more curious still is Bostock's statement that he could only speak with almost equal certainty to the poison bottle containing corrosive sublimate, whereas he had been certain about it containing arsenic. If his tests, as he would later claim, were sensitive enough to detect sublimate in a solution containing only a three millionth part, how on earth was it possible for him not to be certain when he had a bottle saturated with the stuff?

Cross-examined by Mr Topping, Dr. Bostock confessed that he entered upon the examination of the body fluids and organs already under the notion conveyed to him that the deceased had died of poison. He said that he did not believe the gullet and other parts would be affected as the quantity of poison needed to produce death was not large if taken all at once. This bizarre answer beggared the question, if it was large enough to corrode a hole in the stomach why would it not cause corrosion on its way in? Asked how he found the edges of the hole, he answered that the sides easily tore, that they were tender and ragged because they had been handled.

Q : Did it appear to you to be in that state in which Mr Hay has described it, so tender that he could put his fingers through?
A : I should imagine so; I myself easily tore it.

Fairfax Hay had accidentally enlarged it. Bostock had torn it. One wonders how much manhandling the edges of the hole had gone through. Dr. Bostock said he had no personal experience of the operation of the gastric juice, but agreed that it was the opinion of that great authority John Hunter that it would produce the effect of dissolving the stomach, and that there had been ample time between the Friday and the

Sunday for it to have done so.

Topping brought up a new matter. Was Bostock aware that a mixture of arsenic and corrosive sublimate had a perfectly innocent domestic purpose as a bug destroyer? Bostock said he was. 'Frequently used, is it not, for washing furniture with, for the purpose of destroying vermin?' Bostock answered that it may be so, that he believed it to be so. The court now heard for the first time that Angus had requested the medical gentlemen to examine the drawers in his house so that they could see for themselves. Bostock had done so with Dr. Rutter, and after a minute examination thought he could perceive a whiteness about the drawers, though it was not obvious.

Sergeant Cockell announced that that was the prosecution case. In those days, counsel for a prisoner was not permitted to address the jury. The prisoner had the option of either writing his own defence and handing it to the Clerk of Arraigns to read, making a speech himself, or saying nothing at all. He was not permitted to go into the witness box. Angus chose to read his own defence. Facing the jury, he squared up to his monumental task.

'My Lords and Gentlemen of the Jury, from the nature of the crime laid to my charge, I understand the law for wise purposes no doubt denies the assistance of an advocate to speak in my defence. This, to me, is a serious deprivation; but whilst I lament the refinement in this part of the trial, I am compelled to submit to the loss. I will attempt as concisely as I can to inform you of the long progression of this lady's illness, which ended in her death, and at the same time account for the uncommon activity which has been shown by two persons in instigating and carrying on the prosecution against me'.

Angus narrated Margaret Burns' medical history, her electrocution for the dropsy, her state of general ill health. He said that one of the strongest reasons why she was returning to her mother at St. James' Palace in London was that 'she might get her to consult advice, and try if it was possible to relieve her, as formerly, from such a malady'. Her intention to return to her mother so that she might seek medical attention would be 'proved by letter'.

'She would not, on any account, hear of my employing a medical man; her mother must do it; neither was the subject a fit one for me to speak on, either to herself or medical gentlemen on her account; else had I imagined any danger more than formerly, I would have insisted on medical attendance'.

He went on to say that she had been in a debilitated state for several years, had been in ill health all the past winter, and indeed up until the time of her death. It was not to be wondered at, he gave it his opinion, that excessive weakness should rupture the coats of her stomach. Then he came to his explanation of how she had met her death.

'Such very short breathing did not appear till the vomiting had nearly ceased, when a shortness of breath caused her to sit erect, as if something had been suddenly displaced. This, probably, was the time when the coats of her stomach were ruptured. After that the shortness of breath increased, she requested the castor oil to be given of her own accord, in order to try, if possible, to remove the inconvenience. The castor oil I told Mr Vause I had administered, on the morning she died, was given for that purpose. She was still of opinion, that the shortness of breathing was only temporary and would go off immediately. At this time a calmness of breathing took place, and she expressed a wish for wine. Not having any in the house, it was accordingly sent for. In the meantime she lay down on the sofa, and I thought, after the fatigue of such vomiting and shortness of breath, she was going to sleep a little, and that repose would, in some degree, restore her. Not imagining anything like death would ensure, I sat down in an easychair, and after the anxiety I had experienced, not only on my brother's account, who had lately before been deprived of his mental faculties, but also on hers, I fell asleep. In the interim, I understand the cook attended her and returned into the kitchen. During the time I had dropped asleep, the deceased had got from the sofa, in order as I suppose to leave the room, and whether a shortness of breathing or a fainting came over her, I know not, but when the girl came back with the wine, the deceased was found dead, in a recumbent posture by the door as had been described; and when I was awoke, I was quite astonished and confounded, not imagining when I sat down in the chair that anything like death was near, nor did she herself seem to think it at all throughout her illness'.

The poison, he said, was expressly labelled as such. Seven years earlier the moths had materially injured his blankets and woollens, and he had obtained the mixture in order to destroy them. He had also applied it to the floors on which his most valuable carpets lay. If the smallest part had been administered to the deceased, he emphasised, it would unavoidably have been detected seeing how readily Dr. Bostock had distinguished corrosive sublimate from the arsenic in the fluid.

'I would indeed have been one of the most criminal of men had I done that lady an intentional injury in any respect, much less anything to affect her life. The care she took of my children, and the interest she evinced generally, for my domestic concerns as well as my interest, made it my bounden duty to preserve rather than to destroy her existence.'

On the Reverend John Vause and the black puke, he explained that there was no such medicine. It was a term applicable to a disorder terminating in death, as in the case of various fevers, frequently used in Africa and the West Indies. It was nothing uncommon to say 'such a one was carried off with a black puke' meaning the colour of the vomit. Then at last he came to the surgical instrument around which so much controversy revolved. His account of it was not for the squeamish.

'The application of it has been totally misrepresented. It was never intended for any purpose relative to women. As I had studied Bell on the venereal disease, and had cured many venereal cases, it was in these instances that I applied it. The instrument was much longer, and as thin as a knitting needle, and this probe was neither more nor less than to be introduced into men's urethras, in cases of stricture or warts. I proposed it to have been chisel pointed, and Mr Richardson the instrument maker recommended the other as better, and the instrument is not too thick for boring my eldest daughter's ears, but she had an inflammation in her eyes, and I was therefore dissuaded from using it, and that is the reason why her ears were not bored.'

Angus was saying that he had intended boring the ears of his eldest daughter Jane with the same instrument he inserted up mens' penises to treat the strictures caused by gonorrhea, a treatment at the time known as 'sounding'. Jane probably didn't realise how fortunate she was.

Angus concluded with an emotional plea under the full conviction that the 'Great Searcher of Hearts' was satisfied of his innocence:

'Gentlemen, I submit to your judgement, and as you are upon your oath, I call upon you to remember that there has been no satisfactory evidence adduced to prove that this lady was either murdered or poisoned by me, or by any other person whatever. She died by the visitation of God, through excessive vomiting operating on her delicate constitution, without the intervention of any human means. Yet we see how easy a thing it is to accuse. But in this country, thank God, accusation without clear proof avails nothing when a man's life is at stake. If I must die in consequence of this charge which has been brought against me, more from motives of revenge and enmity than to promote the ends of public justice, I will die, with this assurance, that my enemies must give an account to the same unerring God I am to be judged by, and who is more able to estimate the rectitude of their motives than any earthly tribunal. Such an opinion, however, has been instilled into my mind, of the integrity and impartiality of a British Judge, and of a British Jury, that I consider my life safe in their power, well knowing they will not exercise that power unduly, but conscientiously, as they must be hereafter answerable to their God for the use they make of it.'

Probably no counsel could have delivered a more eloquent speech on his behalf. Unfortunately it failed to answer many of the puzzling aspects of the case. Why had it taken so long to wake him? How had he fallen into such a deep sleep only twenty minutes or so after ordering dinner? Why had he done nothing about the body for over two days? Neither had he given a satisfactory explanation for the state of the uterus, or why so many people should have told lies about him.

The first defence witness was Martha Barton from Hunter Street, who had recommended the Grains of Paradise. She testified that Miss Burns had been poorly for twelve months and was inclined to be dropsical. Mrs Barton said that she had a sister who 'died of a dropsy', and was in a position to say that Miss Burns presented the same appearance.

Sergeant Cockell's brief cross-examination for the prosecution had a contemptuous ring to it. He put to her that some persons in pregnancy had symptoms which they often called a dropsy to cover up the fact, and that Mrs Barton clearly believed everything Miss Burns said. She had no firm reply.

She was followed by her married daughter, Elizabeth Jones. Her evidence was so bizarre and contradictory in places that she had Miss Burns deflating and inflating like a balloon.

On Sunday the 13th of March, ten days before the start of the illness that had terminated in the governess' death, Mrs Jones had taken tea at Angus' house. Startlingly, Mrs Jones told the court that Miss Burns was as large then as she had been the February of the previous year.

Q : Are you confident of that, Mrs Jones?

A : Yes, sir, I am confident, for I have been with her in her dressing room.

Q : Did she continue in the same state throughout the year?

A : Yes, sir - I saw no difference, increasing or decreasing, from the February but one before she died, to the time of her death.

Q : Had you any reason to think she was pregnant?

A : No, sir, I never suspected anything of the kind, and I could not think she was.

A few weeks before her death, Mrs Jones had assisted in dressing Miss Burns and had remarked how thin she was. Elizabeth Jones was the first and only witness at the trial to say that Miss Burns looked thin. She went further and explained how she had commented on Miss Burns being so uncommonly flat-bosomed, and not half so plump as she used to be. The jury must have wondered if she was talking about the same woman.

The subject of the management of the house brought a telling interruption from the prisoner. Mrs Jones had just recounted how Miss Burns had every key except to the iron bookcase and Angus' clothes.

'My wife's clothes' Angus interjected, not wishing the court to be under any apprehension that Miss Burns had enjoyed free access to his departed Maria's wardrobe. Elizabeth Jones had seen Miss Burns open Angus' wardrobe where the medicines (and poison) were kept, and had assisted in putting in the clothes after the drawers had been washed with Jacob's Water. Asked why she called it Jacob's Water, she said that was the name Mr Angus gave it. He had recommended her mother try it if she was ever troubled with moths. She had seen him using the water himself but did not take notice of the label on the bottle.

(The contents of the two Jacob's Water bottles had never been revealed by Dr. Bostock. It was the bottle marked Poison Water which contained the corrosive sublimate and arsenic, the mixture which Bostock had affirmed was a bug destroyer).

Miss Burns was then inflated again. Asked to describe her appearance when she saw her laid out on the sofa on the day she died, Elizabeth Jones said she was as large as she was when she was living. Even the slowest and most mentally exhausted member of the jury must have realised that if that was so, she could not possibly have been thin and flat-bosomed.

Cross-examined by Mr Holroyd, Elizabeth Jones agreed that she had not been sent for during Miss Burns' illness in spite of her intimacy with her and living only a quarter of a mile away. Neither was her mother sent for. Considering the inconsistencies of her evidence regarding Miss Burns' size, she escaped very lightly.

The penultimate defence witness was Jane Overhin, Angus' servant of eighteen months back. The reason she had been subpoenaed by the defence soon became clear. She too remembered the drawers being rubbed with Jacob's Water while she was in service, to keep the moths from the clothes. She had visited Miss Burns since leaving Angus' service, and did not believe that she was pregnant.

Cross-examined, she admitted she had said more before the coroner. She was sharply reminded of the incident with the breakfast tray. She said she was never forbidden to take it into Angus' bedroom, that Miss Burns always took it from her. She agreed that she had commented on the great liberties taken by the governess, and asked if she was to be married to the master.

Dr. Carson's moment now arrived. He was the final witness of the trial. It was around midnight and the oil lamps of the crown court in the mediaeval castle cast their eerie glow on the proceedings. Examined by James Scarlet, the good doctor gave it as his opinion that the hole in Miss Burns' stomach had occurred after death. He could not conceive of a poison so acrimonious as to produce a hole of such magnitude without producing other destructive appearances. A hole in the stomach, he maintained, was by no means an uncommon appearance.

Not to be left behind, he now elected to give the court the benefit of his own reading and launched into a highly informed account of three of the eminent John Hunter's cases in which a hole had been found in the stomach after death. One was the case of a man who had been killed by a stroke on the head from a poker and had died instantly. He had eaten a plentiful supper of beer, bread, cheese and meat, and upon the opening of the body, the stomach contents had been found to have passed into the cavity of the belly in contact with the liver and spleen. The other two cases involved a man whose skull had been fractured by a brickbat, and a soldier who had been executed. Dr. Carson had in his hand a piece of paper on which he had copied an extract from Hunter's own account which described the edges of the perforation as 'half-dissolved, pulpy, tender and ragged' - much the same description that had been offered by the medical witnesses for the crown.

Having quoted Hunter, who proposed the gastric juice as the culprit, Carson then proceeded to go one step better and disagree with him. In a long rambling speech, which must have lost everybody in the court, and in which he feverishly name dropped other leading authorities to prove his point, he came to the startling conclusion that water in the stomach at a temperature of ninety degrees, mixed with the common salt taken in food, could cause the stomach to dissolve. He would later be bitterly accused of confounding digestion with putrefaction.

He then moved on to the uterus and immediately placed himself on even more dangerous ground. Gerard, Bostock and Fairfax Hay must have wondered how he was going to explain that away. Carson was ready for them.

'Under these circumstances,' Scarlet asked, 'can you assign any other cause for those appearances, which these gentlemen have thought indicated the recent expulsion of a child?'

This was his moment.

'I think,' he answered, 'that the most probable cause, independent of pregnancy, is a dropsy of the hydatids.'

One can easily imagine the consternation on the faces of his colleagues. Dropsy is a condition characterised by an accumulation of watery fluid in the tissues or in a body cavity. Hydatids are large bladders containing the encrusted larvae of the tapeworm Echinococcus, or sometimes sterile fluid filled cysts produced by infestation with the same tapeworm which is a parasite of dogs. Today hydatid cysts is a rare infectious disease, found in communities where sheep and cattle raising is carried out with the help of dogs. The eggs are excreted in the faeces of the dogs, and if they are swallowed by man in contaminated food or water (or transferred by licked plates and utensils) enter the bloodstream and form cysts, usually in the lung or liver where the blood is much richer. They can take up to thirty years to grow and can become the size of a grapefruit. In 1808, when Britain's agricultural landscape was extensive, the necessity for hygiene little understood, and the link between hydatid cysts, dogs and cattle totally unknown, the prevalence of the disease was far greater. People allowed dogs to lick from their household plates without compunction. The notion of a separate bowl for the family pet would have seemed like an eccentricity from across the channel.

Dr. Carson's defence was ingenious. Deeply flawed, but nevertheless ingenious. He was in effect saying that Margaret Burns had given 'birth' to a huge ovum of tapeworm cysts that had grown in her uterus.

'These Hydatids,' continued Dr. Carson, 'are attached by Pediculi to the internal surface of the womb, and when by an action being excited in the womb, similar to parturition, these Hydatids are expelled, the mouth of the womb is dilated.' He did not believe there would be undue contraction of the uterus after the expulsion.

Sergeant Cockell rose to cross-examine. 'Pray, Dr. Carson, was you originally bred to Physic?' he asked. Carson had originally trained as a Church of Scotland minister. Carson replied truthfully that he was not. He admitted that he had no great experience of midwifery whereas Dr. Gerard could boast a considerable practice. Asked if he had seen a number of uteri, he blew his credibility with a pompous and arrogant answer.

> A : Yes, but in this case, it is entirely a physical question arising from mechanical principles, with which extensive practice has little to do.
>
> Q : Have you ever practised the obstetric art at all?
>
> A : I have not.
>
> Q : And yet you set up your judgement and opinion against the opinion of this gentleman, who has been in practice for thirty years?
>
> A : I may surely be permitted to state the impressions of my own mind?

Sergeant Cockell was not going to let Dr. Carson get away with his impressions. He asked him if in examining the womb he did not see the place where the placenta had been attached? What followed was the trial's most heated exchange.

> A : That which was supposed by these gentlemen to be the place,

I suppose I did see.

Q : Now, I should be glad to know, Dr. Carson, whether a dropsy can generate a placenta?

A : Certainly not.

Q : Then, if you did see that place, where it was supposed the placenta had been attached, what was it that had been attached if it was not the placenta?

A : It might be the attachment of some other substance contained in the womb.

Q : Come, Dr. Carson, I will have an answer! What other substance except the placenta could possibly attach itself?

A : Those I have mentioned are the most probable, the Hydatids.

Q : Will you swear, sir, that that was not the mark of a placenta?

A : I can say, sir, that under the two circumstances, if neither a mortal flooding have taken place, nor any coagulated blood been found in the cavity of the uterus, that a placenta could not possibly have been detached from this womb.

Q : I ask you, sir, whether these appearances could have arisen from anything but a placenta?

A : I think they might. I think they possibly might be what I have mentioned, the attachment of some dropsical hydatids.

Q : Have you heard Dr. Gerard say he could speak with as much certainty to a placenta having been attached, as if he had seen the child born?

A : I do not recollect the expression.

Q : Why, Good God, you were attending and taking notes! You must certainly have heard him say that so evident were the remains of the vessels that he was as certain of the removal of a placenta, and could speak with as much certainty of a child having been born as if he had seen it?

Sergeant Cockell asked him how the womb could have been so far extended in the mouth unless a foetus had been discharged. Pressed,

Carson admitted he really could not say with certainty.

'You never delivered a woman in your life?' Sergeant Cockell put to him bluntly. 'No', came the sorry reply.

Carson was briefly re-examined by James Scarlet, who was able to repair only a little of the damage. Carson had at least seen a uterus dissected before, which Dr. Gerard had not. With that, the evidence came to an end. All that was left was for the judge to sum up and the jury to reach a verdict. The hour was late, well into the morning. Before dawn broke, Angus would know his fate.

Mr Justice Chambre's summing up was largely a reiteration of the evidence, and as such was scrupulously fair. Not for nothing had he earned his high reputation. A hanging judge he most certainly was not. He did however point out that the indictment charged Angus with a number of possible offences, that he had administered the poison himself, that he had persuaded Miss Burns to take the poison, that he had administered the poison to her with the intention of making her miscarry, that he had enticed her to take it for that reason. There was also a fifth charge in the indictment, which he believed came nearer to the fact - that Angus had aided and assisted Miss Burns in taking poison to kill her child. That in itself would still be murder according to the law.

Neither, he said, were they trying the question of whether Miss Burns was delivered of a child or not. It was really almost like trying another and distinct case. If she had not been pregnant, and had still died by an attempt in which the prisoner had been concerned to procure an abortion, he would still be guilty of murder.

With respect to the circumstances of Miss Burns being pregnant, he told the jury that they were put into an unenviable position. 'Who shall decide when doctors disagree?' he quoted a common observation, little knowing that two centuries later his judicial descendants would still be making it.

Regarding the evidence that Angus had used expressions showing he had 'latitudinarian principles' towards abortion, Mr Justice Chambre was inclined to dismiss it. 'I am afraid that in many cases we lay too great a stress upon circumstances of this sort,' he said. Nor did he think that

Angus' possession of the Oil of Savin was a material circumstance, as Miss Burns had not died of that poison. Also in Angus' favour was the fact that the mixture in the poison bottle was not a secret, that it was clearly labelled as poison, and that the deceased herself kept the key to the place where it was kept.

The circumstance which told most against Angus, in the judge's mind, was his conduct in being so continually with the deceased during her illness. It seemed to him extremely odd, and he hardly knew how to account for it, since there were two other women in the house. There was an 'indelicate appearance' in such a state of affairs. He was also inclined to believe that there had been 'more than a common bond' between Angus and Miss Burns.

Turning to the more mysterious elements of the case, he said that the state of the body was extraordinary. How did it happen that she should have been apparently in good health until the Wednesday morning, and after her death on the Friday her stomach should have been found in such a condition? Tests had been applied to the contents and had produced nothing. Furthermore, if a child had been born, it had certainly been very dexterously concealed. Diligent search had been made for it, yet no child had been found, in spite of the fact that appearances indicated the child had come to pretty near its full growth. Mr Justice Chambre was inclined to think that the account of the child having been born, as given by the prosecution, was the more probable one. Strongly suspicious as the circumstances were, however, he thought that the probability concerning the poisoning was in Angus' favour. Then he struck at the very heart of the mystery, and posed the question which must have been uppermost in the jury's minds.

'At the same time one is under considerable difficulty to conceive when it was born. The parlour door was never locked, for instance, and it does not appear that anybody who ever came there ever found any obstacle in going into the room. Why, if they were engaged in administering a medicine of this sort, how could they be sure when it would take effect? The maid servant attends her in the daytime, and no secrecy was observed by her on their part; indeed that would not answer, unless they precisely knew the time when the miscarriage would take place. It was as likely to take place in the daytime as in the night, and he would most likely be as jealous of its taking place then. But in the daytime, it is impossible that this could have happened, and as to its taking place in the night, it is very difficult to conceive how it could; there is no appearance from any circumstances, from the state of the linen, the state of the sofa, the carpet, or anything; there is no circumstance of that sort, which could indicate that at any particular period, the event is likely to have taken place. Then the man was fast asleep at the time the death really happened; for there does not seem to be any possibility that it was either a short sleep or a pretend one. On the contrary, the fatigue he underwent may very naturally account for his falling asleep just at this time. But his being in the room just at that time proves nothing with respect to what had happened; that could not have been the time when she was delivered. How then could he have managed all this, or how could he have conveyed away the child unobserved? I protest, I am unable to explain it'.

He raised another interesting question. If Angus had recourse to the methods of procuring abortion, why had he allowed the child to continue in the womb for so long? Why had he not experimented much sooner? His attitude appeared to be that of kindness and affection and he had always behaved to Miss Burns with tenderness. There was a considerable difference of testimony in the case. Under all these doubts and difficulties, the judge said, he would have great difficulty in finding a verdict against the prisoner. The science of medicine was quite out of his sphere. The jury were as good a judge of the evidence of the learned doctors as he was. He concluded,

'If you are really of the opinion that the prisoner did commit the act with which he is charged, the crime certainly is an enormous one, and the law, justice and humanity ought to be satisfied; but if you entertain any doubt about it, you will of course acquit him, considering that it is better that ten guilty persons should escape than that one innocent man should suffer'.

By the time the judge finished speaking it was nearly half past three on the Saturday morning. The trial had lasted nineteen and a half hours without a break. The summing up had been fair, impeccably so. If the laws of the age had denied Angus the benefit of a final speech by his counsel, Mr Justice Chambre had certainly filled the gap by summing up in a manner which showed that he doubted at least the legal guilt of the prisoner. Angus' jury did not even leave their box. After conferring for a few moments with his fellow jury members, the foreman rose and said that they had found a verdict of 'NOT GUILTY' against Charles Angus.

An acquittal of murder is never the end of a story. Deep suspicion remained, and would ferment even more now that the trial was over. Far too many egos had been bruised and far too many reputations sullied. There was a popular air of indignation among Angus' accusers and a commonly held belief that he had narrowly escaped the gallows because of the evidence of one man - Dr. James Carson. The mounting anger would very soon find its focus on the return of both men to Liverpool, and have deeply unpleasant repercussions.

13   Dr. Carson, Dragon Slayer

'Then home let us hasten, which yet we can see,
For no watchman is waiting for you and for me;
So said little Robert, and pacing along,
His merry companions returned in a throng'.
> 'The Butterfly's Ball'

Some of Angus' fellow prisoners at the assizes were not so lucky. A man of fifty-eight was given fourteen years transportation to Botany Bay in Australia for uttering a forged one pound Bank of England note, the same sentence being given to two others convicted of a similar offence. John Torr, the bigamist with three wives, was fined one shilling and imprisoned for a year, while another bigamist with only two wives was fined a shilling and imprisoned for six months. Six months per extra wife seemed to be the rule of thumb at the Lancaster Assizes of 1808. Transportation for seven years was the cruel sentence passed on John Dobson who had stolen a piece of woollen cloth from a fulling mill. There were four sentences of death passed, one for murder, one for maiming and wounding, one for stealing a horse, cart, gears and harness, and the fourth on a fifty year old woman for stealing five and a half bundles of linen yarn. In the event, all four were reprieved by the judge, and sentenced instead to two years imprisonment in a house of correction. The hangman was therefore not called to Lancaster that autumn. It was probably just as well. Only the year before, ugly scenes had occurred at Newgate when the hangman, James Brunskill, had executed two men whom many in the crowd believed innocent. Such was the tumult of the mob that thirty people, some of them children, were trampled to death. The event was still horribly fresh in peoples' memories.

Angus' return to Liverpool was far from triumphant. He had perhaps avoided the gallows, but he could not escape the stares and whispers of those he had once considered friends and neighbours. He had no intention of staying in Liverpool, in fact he had been considering his retirement from the place even before his arrest. Now, the wish to pack up and return to his native Galloway burnt more strongly in him than ever. There were a number of things he had to take care of first. One was the education of his children who had been living at home throughout his imprisonment under the care of the Biggams. Another was his brother Alexander who had been locked up in the madhouse at Billington for the past eight months. Shortly before his incarceration, Alexander had conceived his second illegitimate child in Liverpool, and that child was now just over a week old. Both his children were christened together at St. Peter's Church on the 2nd of October, being given the names Alexina and Alicia. Whether their father was well enough to attend the christening is not recorded.

The third duty pressing on Angus was to find out what had become of his Jamaican property, St. Faith's Penn. There were, predictably, no letters waiting for him from William. He was not slow in firing off a letter to his errant brother, explaining how he had born his confinement with calm firmness and gone through his trial with the utmost cool composure. 'Conscious of my perfect innocence' he wrote, 'my mind was born up wonderfully under such pressure of affliction'. It was not many sentences later that he was getting down to the nitty-gritty. 'Oh my dear Brother William, under such complicated affliction,' he entreated, 'how is it possible you can reconcile your long silence by your conscience? If my property is in any way improving, your confirmed silence tends no little to show that you have not my peace of mind much at heart, else you would write often, seeing the satisfaction I feel on hearing how the property is conducted and its progress.'

He was back on form. To his nephew Robert Hornell in Antigua, who owed him money, he wrote that 'God in his Gracious Providence so ruled the heart of a just judge and an impartial jury that I was acquitted on both charges of either destroying a child or poisoning the lady'. Then he pressed his nephew to lose not an hour in discharging the sums he owed him.

A drawing of Angus made at the trial by an anonymous artist. Curly hair brushed forward at the front was very fashionable at the time.
(With kind permission of the Lancashire Record Office – Ref QJC1)

The Borough Goal, where Angus was imprisoned during the inquest into Miss Burns' death.

(From a scarce woodcut)

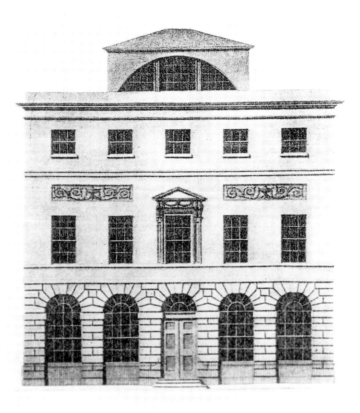

The Liverpool Athenaeum, from which came many of the witnesses at Angus' trial. Angus supposedly disposed of the dead baby on his way to the club.

(With kind permission of the Liverpool Record Office)

Dr. James Carson, defence witness and dragon slayer. A bust in the possession of the Liverpool Medical Institution.

Finart House, Glen App. The 'Lonely Place' to which Angus retired after his trial. It was demolished in the 1940s.

Turnberry Lodge, Ayrshire, where Charles Angus died in 1820.

Charles Angus' last resting place in Kirkoswald graveyard. Buried with him are his only son, Thomas McQuistin Angus, and his daughter Jane.

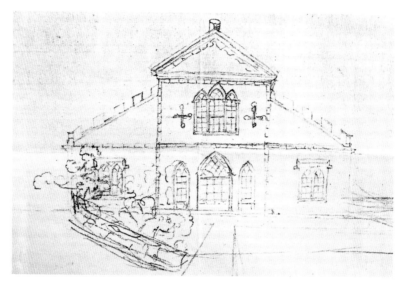

A pencil sketch of Turnberry Lodge, made by Angus' daughter Maria. She would keep the sketchbook all her life.

In not one of Angus' letters after the trial does he mention Dr James Carson.

Angus was not the only one whose reputation had suffered. Thomas Fairfax Hay and Drs. Gerard and Bostock were furious that they had been made to look less than competent at the trial. Gerard and Bostock particularly were highly respected physicians whose authority had been severely eroded by Carson's successful if wildly implausible defence. If Margaret Burns had given birth to a mass of hydatids, what, they asked, in the name of God had happened to them? Why hadn't somebody in the house kept them, or shown them to someone? Why, indeed, after the evidence of both servants and a passionate speech by Angus himself, had Dr. Carson been the first one to mention hydatids? Nobody had raised any of these points at the trial.

Neither was it the first time that Carson had crossed and got the better of his medical colleagues. None of them had forgotten or forgiven an occasion four years earlier when, as a comparatively young and ambitious doctor, he had caused an upheaval at the Liverpool Dispensary. In a scenario that could almost have been lifted from the pages of George Eliot's *Middlemarch*, Carson and a group of his medical friends had led a concerted attack on the old guard at the Dispensary, the tight little body of physicians who saw it as their God-given right to further their careers and social standing by being elected to it year after year, and taken over the institution.

In the bitter storm of resentment which followed, four of the old guard resigned, two of whom were Dr. John Rutter and Dr. Bostock. It was no wonder then that, after Angus' acquittal, these doctors had an even greater score to settle against their colleague.

On the 14th of September, eleven days after Angus had walked free from the crown court at Lancaster, Rutter, Bostock, Gerard and Fairfax Hay were joined by three others, Drs. Joseph Brandreth and John Lyon, and Henry Park, Angus' own family physician. The purpose of this uncommonly large gathering was to examine the ovaries of the uterus. As to why they had not examined them before, they had a ready answer. They were so perfectly satisfied with the other proofs of pregnancy that they did not suppose it possible for such proofs to be called into question. Similarly this had been the reason why they did not examine the breasts. The uterus had been kept in spirit for nearly six months, yet the part to which the placenta had adhered was still rough, and the vessels still discernible. They set about dividing the ovaries and in one of them they discovered what might today be termed 'startling new evidence'. A *corpus luteum* was distinctly observed in one of the ovaries. (A *corpus luteum* is a glandular mass of tissue which forms in a follicle subsequent to the release of an ovum. While they were clearly observable, at that time their purpose was not understood - that purpose being to secrete progesterone, a hormone necessary to maintain pregnancy). This was further proof, as if they needed it, that they were right and Dr. Carson had been wrong.

The next day, a bizarre sequel was set in motion. Fairfax Hay was despatched by stagecoach to London with Miss Burns' uterus bobbing about in spirit with the intention of obtaining affidavits from as many London physicians as possible to the effect that the uterus had contained and excluded a child. He did not take the stomach with him, perhaps because they had universally conceded that they had no case to bolster.

In an action that would be inconceivable today, Fairfax Hay carted the uterus from hospital to hospital, consulting room to consulting room, collecting evidence against a man who had already faced his trial and been found not guilty. If it was merely a face saving operation however it was a resounding success. Three accoucheurs, Thomas Denman, John Haighton and C.M. Clarke, the last of whom was a member of the Royal College of Surgeons and a lecturer on midwifery, all signed affidavits stating that the uterus bore all the marks of having been impregnated. Henry Cline, Surgeon to St. Thomas' Hospital, 'could not conceive of the appearances originating from any other cause'. The uterus was then shown to no less a personage than Astley Paston Cooper, later to be Sir Astley Paston Cooper, one of the most distinguished London surgeons of his day. He had an enormous practice. For many years his annual income would top fifteen thousand pounds, a sum to make most Liverpool physicians' eyes water. Even his servant was said to make six hundred pounds a year showing in patients out of their turn. Astley Paston Cooper stated that although his opportunities of forming a judgement were very limited when compared with those who practised midwifery, he had been called upon to inspect the bodies of several women who had died soon after delivery, and was of the opinion that the appearances he had found were 'similar to those which this uterus and ovarium exhibit'. Finally, it was shown to John Abernethy, Surgeon to St. Bartholomew's Hospital, another distinguished London surgeon whose brusqueness was legendary. Abernethy signed an affidavit claiming that 'the enlarged state and peculiar structure of it (the uterus) can have arisen from no other cause than that of its having contained a child of nearly nine months old'.

Needless to say, Fairfax Hay did not bring back with him (or at least did not admit to receiving) any affidavits to the contrary. A few days later, Miss Burns' much discussed and much probed uterus, in company with its now glowing protector Fairfax Hay, arrived back in Liverpool.

On the 3rd of October, Fairfax Hay appeared before the coroner Thomas Molyneaux with not only the six London affidavits but those of a further seventeen Liverpool surgeons and physicians, plus one from Warrington, hardly the hub of the medical establishment. What the coroner's purpose was is not clear. He had no power to send Angus back for trial. One can only assume that he was anxious to do all he could to help the doctors who had testified for the crown to restore their good names. Among the signatories to the Liverpool affidavits were Fairfax Hay's partner Lucas Reay, and George Coltman, who had given evidence at the trial but on other matters. Now he stated that he had seen both the stomach and the uterus near the end of August that year, and had been able to trace nearly the whole outline of that part of the uterus to which the placenta had been attached. He went further and reinforced his colleagues' opinion that 'some very active agent' was the cause of the morbid appearances in the stomach.

Other signatories included the physicians who had been attached to the Dispensary in its early days, Joseph Brandreth, a keen exponent of the cold water treatment for fevers, and James Worthington, who had unsuccessfully tried to turn Liverpool into a spa town. Two physicians, Robert Lewin and John McCartney had axes to grind. They were among those who had resigned from the Dispensary over Dr. Carson's attack on it four years earlier. They stated that the uterus had 'contained a foetus of nearly mature growth, very shortly before the death of the parent'.

Thomas Christian, the young surgeon who had attended the examination of the body at Angus' house but had subsequently played no part in the proceedings, now laid it before the coroner that he had several times seen uteri from which children had been recently expelled, and was in no doubt that Margaret Burns had been in a state of advanced pregnancy. He also claimed to have seen at least one stomach perforated by the effects of the gastric juice, as described by the famous John Hunter, and that it by no means resembled the aperture in Miss Burns' stomach.

The longest affidavit by far came from another young surgeon, James Dawson, a friend and colleague of Fairfax Hay's. It appears that Dawson had gone so far as to take a blow pipe to the uterus and inflate the blood vessels in order to show that they led to the placenta mark. He did not believe such vessels were required 'for the nourishment and support of hydatids'. He wrote that he had lately had the opportunity of opening the body of a young woman who died from inflammation of the uterus on the fifth day after the delivery of a premature child, and the mark of the attachment of the placenta was 'not more clear, satisfactory and decisive than the mark in this uterus'.

The most intriguing came from Angus' own family physicians, Thomas Traill and Henry Park. Traill was the doctor, we may remember, in whose house Angus had told the assembled company that an instrument inserted into the womb would cause an abortion. Traill had no hesitation in adding his voice to the swell. Henry Park's signature to the great mass of affidavits was not so much remarkable for what he said as for who and what he was. He had delivered all of Angus' three children, and was the closest physician to the family. He was also still technically one of the two executors to the will of Angus' father-in-law, a will which was not yet wound up. Angus may have been trumpeting his right to do what he wanted with St. Faith's Penn in Jamaica, but in reality the titles to the land had not yet been transferred to him. As a trustee, Park could take his expenses out of the estate, in those days scope for much 'self-improvement'. If Angus had been found guilty and hanged, Park and his fellow trustee Thomas Fletcher would have controlled all the assets, a tempting position to be in. By putting his name to a declaration condemning Angus, he was setting his seal on any further doctor-patient relationship. Whether or not he had hoped for a different verdict is another matter. If all of these witnesses had appeared in person at the trial, the sheer weight of the evidence would probably have put the rope around Angus' neck. As it was, the second hearing at the coroner's court was nothing short of a retrial.

Not content with simply salvaging their reputation before the coroner, Rutter, Gerard, Bostock and Fairfax Hay now resolved to go one step further and publish the affidavits along with a spirited defence of their own testimony at the trial. Angus was to have no peace from his accusers. The object of the publication was to maintain fervently that Angus had been guilty all along, and to tear apart in no uncertain measure what they called Dr. Carson's 'most extraordinary evidence'.

It was titled 'A Vindication of the Opinions delivered in Evidence by the Medical Witnesses for the Crown on a late trial at Lancaster for Murder' and ran to eighty-eight pages. It immediately created a torrent of indignation, not only among Angus' friends but among Dr. Carson's supporters now holding the top posts at the Dispensary. In it they stated that when Dr. Carson had first seen the uterus he had expressed no doubt about the pregnancy. (Carson would deny this was the case). Neither, they said, was one word uttered by him about hydatids. They laid before the eager Liverpool public their discovery of the *corpus luteum* in one of the ovaries, and defended their reasons for not having found it before. They gave a graphic account of Miss Burns' symptoms, complaining that the evidence at the trial had not been as full as at the inquest. They doggedly stuck to their belief that Miss Burns had been poisoned, spelling out in far more detail than they had given at the trial the experiments conducted on the poor animals. Finally, they rounded on Dr. Carson's evidence, spending half the publication pulling it apart with considerably more thoroughness than they had dissected Miss Burns.

Then they came to the chief object of their derision - the hydatids.

'If Hydatids had been discharged from the uterus, why were they not produced? The production of them would at once have decided the point. If they had been discharged, either Mr Angus who was with the deceased day and night, or the servants, must have known it. Is it conceivable that he would not have produced them himself, or have called upon his servants to produce them, or at least to prove that they had been discharged? The non-production of these hydatids is to our minds an irrefragable proof that in this case they never existed.'

Dr. Carson's account was so palpably absurd, they said, that it was scarcely worth the trouble of refutation. (Though they were taking eighty-eight pages to refute it). Throughout his evidence he had laboured hard for one purpose only - to serve the prisoner, not to promote or assist in the investigation of the truth. His conduct was 'highly unprofessional'. Such conduct 'could have no other effect than that of destroying all confidence in the man who had recourse to it'. They felt that they would be greatly mistaken if Dr. Carson did not experience the consequence of his proceedings in his future intercourse with a great majority of the faculty of Liverpool - a veiled threat if ever there was one.

Finally, Messrs Rutter, Gerard, Bostock and Fairfax Hay declared that they were not actuated by malice or personal enmity, and had not entered upon such subjects with a view to provoking controversy. One wonders who they were trying to fool. They stated that they would take 'no notice of any reply which would be made to this pamphlet, publicly or otherwise'.

In that, they were hopelessly misguided. None of them could have anticipated the vitriolic nature of Carson's response. The 'Vindications' was virtually an edict against any physician disagreeing with another in open court. Who indeed was to decide when doctors disagreed?

Dr. Carson had been working on his own defence even before the 'Vindications' appeared. Now he produced it, to a town hungry for the next sensation. A sensation it certainly was. Even today, Carson's reply must rank as one of the most astonishing diatribes ever written by a physician. It was by turn defamatory, egotistical, angry, and paranoiac in its content. As an exercise in professional suicide it was nothing short of a masterpiece. There was certainly more wisdom in it than in the 'Vindications', but at the same time it is impossible to escape the feeling that it was penned while its author was having an extremely childish and petulant tantrum. One thing that certainly galled him was the fact that, since the trial, Dr. Gerard had been elected Mayor of Liverpool.

The weighty title 'Remarks on a Late Publication entitled Vindications of the Opinions delivered in Evidence by the Medical Witnesses for the Crown on a Late Trial at Lancaster' belied what lay within. Carson began by saying that the opinions a man delivered upon oath had generally been considered so sacred as not to come within the province of criticism. He stood by his opinions 'by every succeeding reflection' and had become more and more convinced that in every material part his evidence was exactly correct.

Then he launched into a sarcastic attack on the abilities of his colleagues. No part of the substance of the stomach itself had been subjected to chemical analysis, not even the tender part around the aperture. The examination of the intestinal cord was not pursued further than the duodenum. Neither was the gullet examined. They had not even bothered to examine the heart or the head, for if they had done so they might have discovered in the latter that a rupture of a blood vessel had occurred as a result of Miss Burns taking a 'slight false step'. This testament to the delicacy of the female constitution apart, he accused them further of not even looking at Miss Burns' breasts and nipples for an indication of whether or not she had been pregnant. 'It appears that the state of the breasts, which used to be examined formerly for the purpose of ascertaining a present or recent pregnancy, are considered now too vulgar a concern to be thought of worthy of notice by the wise accoucheurs of Liverpool,' he noted. On that account, they had no more right to give an opinion in the cause of Miss Burns' death than the most illiterate person in court.

As for the experiments on the dogs, he condemned them for 'ransacking the vegetable and mineral kingdoms for poisons of every quality and power, and subjecting a number of helpless animals to the severest torture'. In Carson's view, it was not only improbable but almost impossible that any of the corrosive sublimate ever reached the stomachs of the dogs, this being the reason for their failure to find any. Forty drops of liquid, he contended, would scarcely moisten the palm of the hand. It would have combined with the fleshy part of the throat before it reached the top of the gullet, which they should have examined.

'A man might as well search the ocean for the stone he had thrown into the Mersey yesterday, as have searched the stomachs of these dogs,' he pontificated. 'Poisoning is the basest, most cowardly and most cruel of all kinds of murder, and evinces an extreme depravity in the heart that can be guilty of it. The grounds therefore upon which such an enormous crime, so revolting to human nature are to be founded, ought to be of known stability, and not the deceptive quicksand surface of a day's formation over which light and feathery beings may pass with safety, but which will be avoided by the manly steps of the cautious and wise.'

If caution and wisdom were the attributes of Dr. James Carson, then he was soon about to throw them to the four winds. He confessed that his evidence about the hydatids was no more than a 'conjectural opinion' suggested to him at the eleventh hour by Dr. McCulloch, and then descended into shameless melodrama.

'Did the womb afford sufficient proof that it had parted with a child? Here is the tug of war. I have hitherto, single-handed, had to contend with four redoubted knights. But a whole host of new faces have sprung up against me, clad in complete armour and of furious aspect, like the warlike produce of the venomous fangs of the dragon monster, still preserving in their transformation the murderous qualities of their parentage. My opponents knowing this to be the weak part of the fortress have like skilful generals collected all their forces to this point, expecting to take it by storm'.

Sword in hand, Carson the dragon slayer and mixer of metaphors took aim at one of the four 'redoubted knights'.

'Are we now returned to the period of ignorance and bigotry, when all matter of reason and conscience were determined by privileged authorities? Is an end to be put to all individual independence of sentiment by the terrors of an inquisition? It is said that Mr Hay, having placed before these gentlemen the womb, first delivered his own sentiments and then mine. That gentleman is among the very last persons whom I would select for being the vehicle of opinions that required anything like the exercise of proper reasoning'.

Having cut Fairfax Hay down to size, he now set about the entire medical profession. 'We are disposed to consider the Practitioners in London as a different species of mortals, possessing a certain degree of infallibility. This has arisen chiefly from the report of the pupils who issue annually from their classes. These Tyroes, having just emerged from the shop of the Apothecary, with no other knowledge than that of gallipots and pills, after attending the London lectures for a few months come forth finished surgeons and accoucheurs, and exercise their skill upon the lives and limbs of their fellow creatures, with a confidence that can only be equalled by their ignorance.'

A more cautious man might have stopped there, but Carson went on.

'The gentlemen of this town have entered into a combination whose certain tendency and only assignable purpose are to ruin my medical reputation! In all this large collection of Liverpool physicians, surgeons, apothecaries, accoucheurs and common dentists, is there a single name that is known to literature or science? I have never heard that a discovery of the least value has ever been made by one of them, that any obscure point has been elucidated, or that anything has ever been added by any of them to the general stock of human knowledge . . . a system of espionage, such as only could have been supposed to exist under the suspicious tyranny of a Robespierre seems to have fixed its cankering roots in the fair fields of Britain.'

Then it became deeply personal. Dr. Dawson, the young Liverpool surgeon who had provided an affidavit after blowing into the blood vessels of the uterus with a pipe, was a 'most obliging young man' he said. 'I remember when Mr Park (Angus' family physician) more than a year ago read a paper upon the retroversion of the uterus, Mr Dawson, who has never as I understood had much practice in midwifery because, forsooth, he is a very young man and a gallant bachelor, had the good fortune to have seen no less than five cases all tending to confirm the theory of Mr Park - while the oldest practitioner in town had never seen more than one or two. If the good fortune of Dr. Dawson continues, with what an assemblage of wonders will his head at length be stored'.

Liverpool, he claimed, appeared to be most excellently adapted for the residence of those who wished to publish upon medical subjects. (In that, he was right). They needed only to mention what facts and cases they wanted and young surgeons like Dawson and Christian would have them ready made like 'pigeon hole constitutions, adapted to all occasions'.

Dawson was not the only signatory to be selected for a personal attack. Dr. Traill he practically accused of murder. 'Dr. Traill, another very young man, has seen a human uterus in the progressive stages of pregnancy, as he at one period practised midwifery. We are not informed upon what extensive theatre this practice was exhibited. But there certainly must have been an uncommon mortality among the women who fell under his charge. They seem to have died for the purpose of giving him a view of their wombs'.

By this time Carson was well out of control, and well out of order. His reply had ceased to be a defence of his opinions, but a bloody onslaught full of bitterness and self pity.

Finally, he cited his theory of how Margaret Burns had met her death. 'The danger of a sudden transition from the recumbent to the erect posture in cases of debility, especially from the affection of the alimentary canal, as in a cholera morbus, dysentery and putrid fevers, is well known'. He believed she had gone to use the chamber pot in another room but, by the time she reached the parlour door she began to feel the 'frequent effects of an erect posture, a deficient supply of blood to the head, and a diminished action in the brain'. Finding herself going, she fell against the corner of the room. The prolonged faint terminated in death.

He did not endeavour to explain how a woman who had made a startling recovery from whatever had afflicted her, who had just ordered lunch, and sent one of the servants to the other side of Liverpool for wine, suddenly died from standing up too quickly.

Whose reputation had been ruined by this poisonous if at times very lucid publication was quite obvious. In attempting to slay the dragon monster, Dr. Carson had fallen on his own sword, destroying any chances he might have had to advance himself in the town. Yet in many ways he had been correct. The examination of Miss Burns' body had been appallingly deficient. He had given evidence for the defence in good faith and under oath. It would have been a sad day for justice if one doctor could not disagree with another when the shadow of the noose lay around a man's neck.

In the Donellan case, which bore a number of interesting parallels, one doctor had testified for the defence against six for the prosecution. Captain Donellan had been accused of poisoning his young brother-in-law Sir Theodosius Boughton with laurel water, yet no poison had been found in the body. The corpse in fact had been in such an appalling state of decomposition that the search for poison had been singularly half-hearted. In spite of this, Captain Donellan was hanged. Perhaps because of this retribution, no obloquy had been heaped at the door of the one doctor who had gone against all of his medical colleagues. Ironically, he was none other than the great man who had been set on a pedestal at Angus' trial - the famous John Hunter.

The matter was not allowed to rest with Carson's Remarks. The young Liverpool surgeon and gallant bachelor James Dawson immediately rushed into print, fuelling the controversy even further. He felt aggrieved at Carson's efforts to injure his character and ridicule him. Such 'offensive and defamatory paragraphs' had surely been written in one of those 'paroxysms of frenzy' that had seized Carson since the trial. 'You have represented me as a very young man - you have not the advantage very greatly over me, sir, in respect of age, certainly not at all in respect of experience. You despise professional experience, when put in competition with your so much vaunted 'mathematical learning and mechanical philosophy'! Your folly, vanity and rashness have involved you in a dilemma out of which you will never be able to extricate yourself'.

He then threatened libel proceedings by saying he was seriously considering appealing to the justice of his country for redress.

In this angry pamphleteering war, it took a fourth and final word to bring a note of sanity to the affair. A Dr. Campbell of Kendal had attended the trial but had played no part in it. His 'Reflections', published after everybody else had had their say, contained the acknowledgement that justice could never be administered when strong prejudice prevailed. If the example which the medical witnesses for the Crown had set were to be repeated and acted upon, then there would be an 'entire revolution in the administration of justice in England, as far as medical testimony was concerned'.

Even the *London Medical Review* came to Carson's defence, accusing Fairfax Hay, Gerard and Bostock of acting 'neither wisely, cautiously, nor charitably', and describing Carson's part as 'tending in a most useful way to counteract the too bold and consequently dangerous opinions which the examiners of the body held out to the coroner and the public'.

For Angus, this continuing war was intolerable. On the 28th of November, 1808, he resigned his membership of the Athenaeum, and during the winter months placed his two daughters in a boarding school near St. Helens, an establishment which rejoiced under the name of Parr Hall, or Mrs Grundy's School for Young Ladies. St. Helens was becoming a popular locale for the setting up of boarding schools, away from the smoke and the grime of the northern industrial towns. With his son Thomas, now turned five, and his epileptic brother Alexander, whom he hoped might be cured by a return to his native air, Charles Angus left Liverpool, a saddened and broken man.

He left behind him a town that was rapidly expanding, that had torn off the shackles of the slave trade and been forced to come to terms with a new and enlightened age. He also left a mystery that would occupy the minds of its inhabitants for many years afterwards. For all the words spoken at the inquest and the trial, for all the words written in anger upon his acquittal, hardly a glimmer of light had been cast on the dark deeds enacted behind the parlour door of Number Two, Trinity Place - if deeds they were.

14 Aftermath

Angus' departure for Scotland was not so much a return to the bosom
of his family as it was a journey into exile. Through his father had remarried many years before, and Angus enjoyed a good relationship with his
stepmother, he chose not to settle in Stranraer but further up the coast
into Ayrshire. The place he chose was just about as far from anywhere as
one could find on that rocky and barren coast, and just about as far from
Liverpool in tempo as it was possible to imagine.

Finart House was one of the bleakest residences in a district
stained with the blood of perpetual feuds between the Earls of Cassilis
and their hereditary rivals, the Kennedys of Bargany. It was a gloomy
place, positioned below gloomy hills, set well back from the shore up
Glen App as though smugly turning its back on the sea. Above it to the
south, on the edge of Hagstone Moor, the road avoided it by a half a
mile going straight to Ballantrae, the name lovingly romanticised by
Robert Louis Stevenson who transplanted the settlement on the Solway
Firth. Ballantrae was then a busy town, the trade of smuggling having
taken the place of the ancient custom of cutting throats. But it wasn't just
the blood of clan feuds and family rivalry that stained the soil of that grim
region. It was an altogether darker and more malevolent history, for it
was here, in a cave just beyond Bennane point, that the infamous canni-
bal Sawney Beane and his extended family once dined on the pickled
limbs of travellers whom they waylaid. They were all dead now and had
been dead well over a century, but the hideous screeches of that hellish
brood and the anguished wails of their victims would forever carry on the
wind. It comes as no surprise that the previous owner of Finart House,
one of the Kennedy clan, had gone insane there.

Angus had rented Finart House ostensibly for a year, but he ended
up staying there for nearly four and a half. It is clear from his letters that
he did not relish staying in such a remote habitation. 'Parting with my

infant children and my own house I had set down in for life, as I had once imagined, to retire to this lonely place with an insane brother,' he wrote to his nephew, 'would have put many beside themselves,' There was one little area of happiness in his life. Thomas was a fine thriving boy who at the age of five could read any English book put into his hands. It was Angus' intention to continue to educate Thomas himself, before sending him away to Edinburgh to complete his education.

A Writ De Lunatico Inquiriendo had been petitioned for on behalf of Alexander by both Angus and his father. It effectively meant that his entire property was put under the order of the Lord Chancellor of England, who decreed a reasonable sum for his maintenance. It throws an incredibly charitable light on Angus that, in an age when epileptics were frequently left to rot in asylums because they were an embarrassment to their families, he should take his sick brother to live with him at Finart House and to take care of him almost single handed. It would seem even more charitable had Alexander's estate not been in the region of twenty-three thousand pounds, at a time when Angus was professing to be hard up. Angus was bitter about the fact that he had sold his furniture in Liverpool at a great loss, and was now out of pocket over his decision to send his two daughters away to boarding school.

Alexander continued to have fits, despite the return to his native air. Fifteen months into the tenancy, on Monday the 19th of June, 1810, at five o'clock in the morning, Alexander was seized by a particularly violent fit. Between the hours of five and ten he had four fits in succession, his breathing became laborious, and froth started to come up at his mouth and nose. At quarter past eleven, he died, expiring in 'the most placid manner' according to Angus. His corpse was conveyed to Angus' father's house in Stranraer, and on the following Saturday it was interred there. Old William Angus, the barber of Stranraer, was the beneficiary. He gave up hairdressing and took to property speculation, something of a hobby among the financially well off in those times. It is likely that because Angus enjoyed a good relationship with his father - one of the few people in his family he still enjoyed any kind of relationship with (he had fallen out with the Biggams since the trial) - that some of the money went his way.

Not long after, Thomas was packed off to Edinburgh to continue his education. Angus was now alone at Finart House. When the wind howled up Glen App, it must have been an eerie place. Infrequently there came letters from his children, even more infrequently from his mother-in-law Jane Williams. Nothing at all came from St. Faith's Penn. 'You keep me starving in the midst of plenty' he wrote his brother William. 'To be wronged by a brother is the most painful of all wrongs'.

He would go to Jamaica just as soon as he could. There is no documentary evidence that he ever did. He continued to write to his nephew, complaining about dishonoured bills, bemoaning the fact that he was hard up.

Parting with his young daughters had been painful for him, for them even more so. Parr Hall boarding school in St. Helens, where they were doomed to spend their adolescent years, was an ugly looking establishment. Its male principal, Mr Grundy, was a mean, avaricious, bad-tempered individual and a womaniser. His wife, who reputedly had never known a moment's happiness since marrying him, was a drunk. Together, this pair, who would have given Charles Dickens some splendid material, presided over an educational facility which Angus was wont to refer to as a 'superior boarding school in the country'. Six months board for each of his daughters was costing him fifteen guineas. This, however, only included instructions in geography, 'with the use of the globe'. Other lessons, such as writing and accounts, dancing, drawing, French and music all cost extra, as did their seats in chapel for which Angus was charged six shillings. With clothing on top of this, the bill for both his daughters in June 1814 came to over seventy four pounds.

Angus complained at feeling the pinch. Frugality became him, and he wrote expressing his annoyance at the extra expenses, on one occasion requesting that they gave up dancing, on another that they discontinued singing. Only his daughters' entreaties and the humble grovelling of the Grundies swayed him from carrying out his economy drive. In one letter, Maria, who always addressed him as 'My dear Father' and signed herself 'Your affectionate daughter', begged him not to worry about the trifling expense caused by their need to attend a public ball at the Fleece

Inn, St. Helens. She then promptly requested twenty-seven yards of cambric muslin, eight yards of flannel, nine yards of diaper, fourteen yards of linen and six pairs of stockings for each of them. The pill was sweetened by their hopes that he might be able to travel to St. Helens to be there with them. Fortunately for Angus, Mr Grundy mislaid the letter - perhaps deliberately - and the invite didn't arrive until the ball was over. Presumably Jane and Maria had to make do with what gowns they had.

Thomas was also proving to be an expense. But at least he was a boy, for whom education was considered far more vital. For some unexplained reason, he too ended up at Parr Hall, under the care of the Grundies, who observed that he did not exactly measure up to the behaviour of a gentleman's son. The fact that Thomas was the only boy in a boarding school full of girls may have played some small part in that assessment. He was not there for very long when Mr Grundy found him an alternative school, this time for young men, but near enough to him to return to Parr Hall and take tea with his sisters on Sundays.

Around that same year, 1814, Angus moved from Finart House and buried himself away in an even more wild and desolate spot, giving every appearance of hiding from the world. Curghie was back over the border in his native Galloway. Even today it is no more than a farm and a cluster of cottages near the very tip of the Mull of Galloway, where seven currents meet at a lonely headland and the sea perpetually roars. Above the din, the only other sounds are those of the seabirds which nest in the perpendicular cliffs, and which wheel, battered by Atlantic winds. The farm at Curghie where Angus stayed was owned by one of the MacDowalls of that district, who may well have been a relation of Angus' natural mother Janet McDowall. Angus stayed at Curgie for at least three years. If he did not enjoy solitude, he certainly had plenty of time to grow accustomed to it.

With birds and cattle for his companions, he became almost reclusive. In 1817 he was forced to face up to the problem of what to do with his daughters when they left school. He did not want them to come and live with him, and wrote to his mother-in-law Jane Williams in London asking her to give them a home. Jane Williams took a long time to reply.

When she did, it was cool and to the point. She said that it would break their hearts, and that she could not possibly consider it. She also took the opportunity of criticising him heavily for keeping up animosity towards his sister Mrs Biggam, who had caused a family rift by demanding two thousand pounds of his father's twenty thousand inheritance. It went much deeper than that however. Mr Biggam had since died, but six years earlier she had requested three thousand pounds of it so that he could get out of trade and become independent. Angus had advised his father not to part with a penny of it. She was well deserving of double the sum, according to Jane Williams, who called Angus' attitude both cruel and un-Christian.

Angus was therefore obliged to have his daughters return. It can't have been very pleasant for them, coming home to a father who had so callously tried to dispose of them. It may have been the need for extra room that drove him to leave Curghie and move yet again, this time to Turnberry, back on the Ayrshire coast. The tiny village of Turnberry, now a golfers' mecca, had a romantic setting. Thomas McQuistin, Angus' father-in-law, very probably named his house in Jamaica after the place because of family connections with the area. Reputed to be the birthplace of Robert the Bruce, it stood on a sandy coastline from every part of which could be viewed the beautiful prospect of the Firth of Clyde, landlocked it seemed on all sides by the Island of Bute, the Island of Arran, Kintyre, and the not very far off coast of Ireland. Completing the grandeur of the spot was the noble rock of Ailsa Craig, thrusting from the sea like some strange ethereal fairy isle round which mist often clung in motionless ribbons of ghostly grey.

Turnberry Lodge, a gothic house on a hump of land near the sea, was to be Angus' last address, the final step in his 'journey through life'. Jane and Maria had grown up into attractive and educated young women, well able to hold their place in polite society. It has to be said that in spite of his obsession with counting the cost of the smallest articles, Angus at the end of the day did not skimp when it came to his children's education. He gave them the best he could. Maria was fond of painting and drawing, and one day she took her sketching book and sat in the garden of Turnberry Lodge, and drew the house. It was a plain child-like drawing, but she paid close attention to the arched and mullioned windows and to the two castellated wings, as well as the pair of crosses carved into the upper storey. She would keep that sketchbook all her life.

The dawn of the year 1820 saw the death of the old mad king, George the Third. The previous summer had been one of intense heat and political agitation. It had seen a force as large as Napoleon's at Waterloo converge on St. Peter's Field, Manchester, in protest against hunger, squalor, shrinking wages and lost jobs. What resulted in the Peterloo massacre had brought the spirit of French revolutionary fervour to the green fields of England. Now, as the bell of St. Pauls tolled through the London fog for George the Third's funeral, thoughts turned to the succession, and to an eight-month-old child, Victoria. It would be another seventeen years before she would sit on the throne, but an England was already passing away.

At Turnberry Lodge, in what the English still referred to as North Britain, Angus presided over the marriage of the first of his daughters, Jane, to William Crawford, the son of a local doctor at Littleton. She was eighteen years old. One person who was not invited to the wedding was the children's grandmother, Jane Williams. Angus' mother-in-law was not even told of the marriage, and only found out by accident some time later. Not surprisingly, she was extremely indignant. The bad blood had always been there, but since the trial it had been worse. The fact that Jane never wrote and told her personally may have been down to Angus. Maria kept in touch sporadically, penning her letters in the most beautiful copperplate handwriting, but Jane kept a studied silence.

Spring came, and the lush and rich carpet of grass which went down almost to the very sea mark became studded with flowers. Certainly Angus walked on that peaceful beach, looking out on the balmy evenings with the breeze in his face at the surrounding islands. Did he think back over the events of his life, to his arrival in Liverpool as a young man, to the tall ships, to his marriage to the thirteen year old Maria, to the happier days when as a young ambitious merchant he had put up for sale pickled salmon of high perfection, Scotch carpets, Holland Geneva and fine brandy from his premises in Mersey Street? If so, he must also have reflected on the tragic events that had delivered him from the gallows, and on the hand of fate that had delivered him safely from them, giving him twelve years to see his children grow into fine young adults.

On the 21st of May, 1820, he died. He was only fifty-three. He was buried in the parish cemetery at Kirkoswald, where his grave still stands today. Carved into the stone is the proud epitaph TO THE MEMORY OF CHARLES ANGUS, FORMERLY MERCHANT OF LIVERPOOL. It would not have displeased him.

Dr. Carson, who more than anyone else had been responsible for giving Angus those twelve years (with the help of a few hydatids) never shook off his association with the case. He filled the office of Physician to the Workhouse and Fever Hospital in Liverpool, to the Pauper Lunatic Asylum, and to the Military Hospital. When the chair of medicine at the University of Edinburgh fell vacant, he applied for it, but was unsuccessful. He also applied for the same chair at the University of Glasgow but was similarly rejected.

He remained unorthodox and controversial to the end, engaging in a series of experiments to determine how much contractile force could be exerted by the lungs. This resulted in the peculiar discovery that the force in an ox was more than sufficient to balance the weight of a column of water eighteen inches in height, and in a dog one of ten inches. These bizarre tests led him to believe that in some tubercular diseases it might be possible to open the pleura, collapse a diseased lung, and keep it collapsed while a reparative process went on. This plan was put into operation by another doctor at Carson's request. An incision was made between the sixth and seventh ribs, but the lung failed to collapse and the patient died a month after the operation. Dr. Carson did not give up, and in another case suggested cutting into the substance of the lung itself. This was tried, but profuse haemorrhaging resulted, and within a few days the patient was dead.

Undaunted, Carson hit on a more novel idea. With the intention of giving his patients the advantage of inhaling condensed air, he began to send them down into the River Mersey in a diving bell which he kept at the pier head, allowing them to remain for some time underwater in it. These experiments excited a great deal of curiosity, and the plan had a fair trial, but with no great success.

Carson's next venture was more a scientific one than a medical one, but then he had always been a scientist at heart. He proposed a more economical method of slaughtering animals so that their blood was not drained off and wasted. Some butchers in the town were encouraged to kill beasts by blowing air into their veins instead of cutting their throats. Decades later, many elderly people in Liverpool would still recall with some fondness the juiciness and the fierce red colour of the meat of Dr. Carson's 'scientifically' slaughtered animals. Like so many of Carson's ideas, it did not catch on.

His most spectacular case involved what was probably the first tracheotomy carried out during epilepsy. The unfortunate subject was a gentleman who was dining at a nearby hotel, and who, to the discomfiture of the waiter, suddenly floundered off his chair in what seemed a fit of choking. Dr. Carson was called for, and he wasted not a minute in summoning the nearest surgeon, who was instructed to cut directly into the patient's windpipe. The operation was carried out when suddenly, to the dismay of Dr. Carson and the surgeon and all present, the patient jumped up spluttering as well as his impaired vocal cords enabled him, 'Who's cut my throat? Where's the man that cut my throat?' In spite of the patient's recovery, Dr. Carson never advised tracheotomy during epilepsy again.

The *Dictionary of National Biography* has him dying in Sutton, Surrey. This is wrong. He retired to Green End, a tiny leafy hamlet near what was then the village of Prescot, Lancashire, where in 1843 he died of diabetes.

Angus' children enjoyed mixed fortunes. Thomas, the youngest and the only boy, was to lead a tragically short life. He was sixteen when his father died, and the following year he made his will, preparatory to voyaging across the Atlantic, a sad but necessary precaution in those times even for a teenage boy. It seems to some extent he planned to follow in his father's footsteps for that summer he was with a merchant ship in Bahia on the coast of Portuguese Brazil, hoping to soon set sail with two hundred and three cases of sugar and one hundred and fifty bales of tobacco. While he was in Bahia, an English sloop of war sailed in with a Portuguese-owned slave ship as a prize (Portugal had not abolished its slave trade) creating so much tension that it was dangerous for the English to go out after dark. Now that their father was dead, he had taken on the role of a faithful protector and friend, and was especially devoted to his sister Maria. He wrote to her, telling her that he dreamt about her every night. In one of his dreams he fought and killed a young man called Fishbourne, possibly a suitor, who had 'disturbed her repose'.

The gallant young bachelor ended up on St. Faith's Penn in Jamaica, which he had inherited. The property which had caused his father so much anguish brought the most accursed luck to Thomas. He died there at the age of twenty-one, almost certainly carried off by the fever. His body was brought back across the Atlantic, and he was buried alongside his father in Kirkoswald cemetery. Maria, needless to say, was devastated by his death.

Maria by this time had another protector. She had since become married to a Stranraer man, Lieutenant Nathaniel Taylor, whose father had once collected taxes on the use of hair powder in the town. A magistrate and a political Liberal who years later would be a zealous advocate for the Great Reform Bill, it would be said of Nathaniel Taylor that he was of a kindly and warmhearted disposition, had a hearty greeting for everyone, was mild and unobtrusive, and ever ready to support the cause of the weak and oppressed. In short, she married a good egg. They lived for a number of years in Observatory House, Stranraer (now incorporated into the North West Castle Hotel) which had been built for Sir John Ross the arctic explorer and which they rented from him. Later they moved to Belmont House, not far from the town, where they brought up sixteen children. Many of the descendants of these children are now living in America.

Maria died on the 7th of July, 1859, at the age of fifty-six. The reason for her death was put down as softening of the brain. She lies today in the Taylor family tomb in the private graveyard of Lochinch Castle.

Jane, the eldest of Angus' three children, did not enjoy such a fruitful life but she certainly enjoyed the longest. Her husband became a doctor but died in Linlithgow after only six years of marriage. Tragically, his death occurred within two months of her brother's in Jamaica, and their funerals must have taken place around the same time. Now widowed, Jane moved with their only son into Observatory House with her sister Maria and her husband Nathaniel, and there she lived for a number of years before moving to Edinburgh. Aunt Jane, as she became known to Maria's expanding family, also took to property speculation with part of a heritable bond taken out by Angus and which had matured on his daughters' marriages. She married again in 1840, after fourteen years of widowhood, this time to a surgeon in the Royal Navy, Alexander Paterson. But she outlived him too. She retired to Girvan, a small town on the Galloway coast, where she took a house in Harbour Street. There, Aunt Jane saw out the rest of her days.

At ten minutes past midnight on the 28th of December, 1869, she died suddenly of a stroke. She was the last person to have been in the house at Trinity Place on that fateful day in March sixty-one years ago. She had been a six-year-old girl then, old enough to have heard and seen and known. One wonders what memories she took with her. What, for instance, were the children doing that morning when Betty Nickson went to Everton to fetch the milk and cream, and did not take them along? Jane went to her grave, and the mystery remained.

It is tempting also to wonder if she ever returned to Liverpool and to Trinity Place in her later years. If she did, she would have found the house still standing and still occupied. But she would scarcely have recognised the neighbourhood. The mansions of St. Anne Street, in her childhood days, had been home to the crème de la crème of Liverpool society. It was to this society that her father had aspired, and from which he had been cast. Sadly, by the time Victoria ascended the throne, the street had already begun to show signs of decay. The old families started to drop off one by one, by death and by removal, until it became nothing more than a thoroughfare. Shops opened, the fields between St. Anne Street and the village of Everton were brought into the market for building, and the whole district began to take on a shabby second rate commercial character. Where Margaret Burns had once walked with the children through long grass and past scented honeysuckle there now sprung up row upon row of monotonous cottages. Insidiously, a grey blanket of Victorian ugliness obliterated a corner of Georgian England, and a world disappeared.

Trinity Place survived well into the present century, its respectability long faded. At the turn of the century Number Two was still in private occupation, but by 1912 it had become a shabby lodging house. Still it went on, like an actress unwilling to leave the stage, until the Second World War when, known as the Mohamed Sultan Lodging House, it had completely lost all of its former character.

In 1941, Hitler's bombs fell on Trinity Church. After the war, it was rebuilt, but fire destroyed it again. This time there was no respite. In the great clearing operation, Number Two, Trinity Place was finally razed to the ground and swept away.

15   What Really Happened?

I discovered the Angus case through the chance acquisition of a copy of the trial transcript, now extremely scarce, but which sold in Angus' day for the princely sum of five shillings. From this yellowing item I set out in search of a man about whom I knew little, for trials rarely tell the whole truth. The quest led me to record offices and libraries, where parish registers, wills, newspapers of the period and contemporary medical pamphlets helped me to put some of the flesh back on the bones. The real breakthrough came, however, when my path crossed with that of another Angus researcher, Peter Robson, who lives in Yorkshire. He was not writing a book, but researching his family history, for he is Angus' great great great grandson, a descendant of the second daughter Maria and her husband, Lieutenant Nathaniel Taylor of Stranraer. A treasure trove of personal letters, family documents and a contemporary portrait of Maria McQuistin, Angus's child bride, were passed down to him on the death of an elderly relative. The portrait now hangs in pride of place on Peter's wall, and the letters form part of a collection that spans his ancestry through two and a half centuries.

The pot of gold was Charles Angus' letter book containing a copy of almost every letter he wrote from 1800 to 1812, covering his marriage, his slave-trading misadventures, and the periods before and after his trial. Unfortunately, although meticulously kept, the book offers no clue to the mystery. The letter of Wednesday 23rd of March 1808 to his nephew in Antigua states 'Uncle Alex is still ill, family well' - there is no mention of Miss Burns' dramatic illness. It was the last letter he entered until after the trial. No copy of any letter exists to St. James' Palace in London informing his mother-in-law of the untimely death of her only surviving daughter. Following his acquittal, he consistently maintains his innocence, denying he played any part in poisoning her, denying there was ever a child.

When I first met Peter, we discussed the possibility, suggested by a solicitor friend, that the case had been in fact 'got up' against Angus, not by Richard Statham and Sarah Lawson but by two prime movers with far more to gain from Angus' execution. Those two individuals were the executors of Thomas McQuistin's will, Henry Park and Thomas Fletcher. In spite of Angus' protestations to the contrary, the will was far from completely wound up even at the time of Margaret Burns' death. Angus had complained bitterly over the years that it seemed to be 'in the ecclesiastical courts for ever', and indeed eight years was not an unusual length of time to wait, especially when the estate involved overseas property. Angus had a hard enough job simply finding out how much the property was making and how many slaves were on it at any given time. It was not until September 1810, two years after the trial, that Angus wrote to his brother William telling him that he had just returned from a trip to England with his father and that he had finally been granted the title deeds to the property. Even then we can't be absolutely certain that Angus was telling the truth - he had gilded the lily too many times. Angus, on his wife's death, controlled all of her assets, yet it would not have been impossible for the trustees to create obstacles if they had resented his sudden inheritance. So were they in any position at all to influence the testimony of witnesses?

Henry Park, as we know, had delivered all three of Angus' children. He was one of the oldest and most respected physicians in Liverpool. To clothe him in the garb of a crooked trustee, intent on depriving Angus' children of their father's money, is to cast him in the role of a malefactor of Dickensian proportions.

Of Thomas Fletcher's character we know much more, because he privately printed and circulated his autobiography many years later at the age of seventy-seven. From it one learns that he was no innocent at looking after other people's inheritances. By the time he replaced Richard Statham as an executor of Thomas McQuistin's will, he had already benefited from the experience of being trustee to the Rivington Estate near Manchester, a country property left to a young man who had not yet come of age. Fletcher records that it was an 'arduous undertaking' since he had to keep the estate together while paying off large debts run up by his uncle, the testator. It is heartwarming to discover that when the young man finally came of age, 'after some inconveniences and privations, he was enabled to maintain his rank and station in the county as a worthy country gentleman' due to Fletcher's guardianship.

Fletcher's life was dogged by debt. In 1800, when Angus' father-in-law appointed him, he owned a share in the ill-fated mercantile house of France, Poole and Fletcher, Jamaican merchants. That winter had been one of considerable commercial distress, especially in the West Indies. The great stagnation was in the sugar markets where prices fell dramatically. Fletcher had a salary of £300 per annum, and believed himself to be worth about £9000, but lost over half of this as a consequence of the firm's bad debts. He acquired a fourth share in a new concern, but was eventually forced out by one of the other partners when he could not bring in more capital.

The great controversy which surrounded Fletcher revolved around his position as one of the trustees of the Liverpool Dock Estate, set up to fund the extension and development of the docks which, by the 1820's, were accommodating as many as ten thousand vessels in a year and still expanding. The Dock Committee on which Fletcher sat were suspected during that period of all manner of frauds and abuses, many of a serious nature being ultimately discovered. Although Fletcher was never charged with anything, the official report stated that 'neglect, waste and extravagance have long prevailed in the disposal of the funds of the Dock Estate'. Fletcher became bankrupt in later years, only to be bailed out by his closest friends.

There is certainly a dramatic irony in the picture of a debt -ridden fellow merchant and Angus' family physician moving secretly in the background, conspiring to make his last walk a much more fatal one than his morning stroll to the Athenaeum. It would be a wonderful scenario in a novel of the period - the wicked executors, the children red-eyed and frightened and cowering in a dark corner, their innocent father mounting the gallows with a prayer on his lips and a stout heart. There is, unfortunately, no evidence of their involvement, other than Henry Park's willingness to put his name to the 'Vindications' after the trial. Angus may have been many things but he was no fool. Had they designs on the estate, or had they been conspiring in any way, he would have known it and would certainly have had something to say in his letters. He was not slow to blame people for his downfall. It must therefore remain a tempting, if insubstantial, theory.

Is it possible then, from the evidence given at the trial and from other circumstances, to know what really happened in Angus' parlour during those three days in March almost two centuries ago?

The Angus case is a rubik cube of a murder mystery. Not because there are a host of suspects, but because there are a host of unanswered questions. Whichever way you turn it, the solution seems strangely elusive. Was there in fact a murder at all? If Margaret Burns was poisoned, did she take it herself or was it administered? Did she give birth to a child? When was it born, and what happened to it? And there are two which override them all. If Angus did administer something to Margaret Burns to make her abort, why did he not do so much sooner, much earlier in her pregnancy? And who was a party to the disappearance of the child? These matters perplexed the judge at Angus' trial, and must be addressed in the search for any answer to the mystery.

Let us dispense with the hydatids straightaway. As ingenious as Dr. Carson's theory was (and it may have gone a long way to saving Angus' life) it falls down on so many scores - not least of which is the fact that a hydatid cyst usually forms in the lungs or liver, and cannot, under any circumstances, generate a placenta. I think there can be little doubt that given the weight of the evidence, that Margaret Burns did give birth to, or miscarry, an almost fully grown child.

The evidence that she was pregnant was far stronger than the evidence she had been poisoned. This was undoubtedly the weak link in the chain. It was weakened even further by the second part of Dr. Carson's defence, namely that the perforation in the stomach might have been caused by the digestive action of the gastric juice operating after death.

It is a delicious concept, that cocktail of mucus, protein-digesting enzymes and hydrochloric acid turning on its creator like some

Frankenstein's monster, and making for itself a meal of the very organ in which it was produced. Unfortunately, it does not do any such thing. Dr. Carson was wrong in both parts of his defence. While the possibility was certainly entertained at the time, the plain fact of the matter is that the body decomposes but the stomach does not digest itself after death.

In two strokes, Angus' defence, as presented at the trial, can be wiped off the board. This is a long way from saying that it makes the prosecution case any the stronger. Dr. Carson was absolutely, unassailably right about one thing. The post mortem examination of Miss Burns was an appallingly deficient and unprofessional examination. Even to call it that is being immensely charitable. It is almost inconceivable that Fairfax Hay and Drs. Rutter and Gerard failed to look at Margaret Burns' breasts for further confirmation of advanced pregnancy. Yet apparently, to a man, they failed to do so. It is equally inconceivable that in trying to establish a case of poisoning by some corrosive agent, they failed to look at the one place where they would have found evidence of it having been taken - the throat. Yet again, to a man, they failed to do so. They have left to posterity, despite all their efforts, such an inadequate autopsy - even by the standards of the time - that from their endeavours we can now never know for certain what killed the poor lady.

It is possible that Margaret Burns died of natural disease. The most probable cause of Miss Burns' death is a perforated gastric ulcer. Just as duodenal ulcer is now a major disease afflicting young and middle-aged men, in the nineteenth century, when duodenal ulcer was rare, it was gastric ulcers which were more common, probably because of poor diets. Perforated gastric ulcers often carried off young women in their twenties in a matter of hours, through haemorrhage or perforation. There was nothing extraordinary or mysterious about them, and the apertures they create have nothing whatsoever to do with any self-digesting properties of the gastric juice. Nowadays, perforated gastric ulcer can be operated on quite simply.

A consultant surgeon explained to me, rather colourfully, that a perforated gastric ulcer can be compared to the assassination of President Kennedy - it is such a sudden and dramatic event that you always remember what you were doing and where you were when it happened. It could be that Miss Burns had had a large and benign ulcer (one that was not cancerous) for some months, with no more symptoms other than loss of appetite, loss of weight and a little anaemia. She was, in fact, described as pale and sallow.

Perforated gastric ulcer often comes on during a meal. It is likely, therefore, that the perforation in Miss Burns' stomach actually occurred during the breakfast of the Wednesday morning. Remarkably, a patient can survive for forty-eight hours, with the stomach contents extravasated among the intestines. Vomiting, dehydration, extreme thirst and bad breathing are all symptomatic. Urine is not passed because it is not made - peritonitis has set in, and the body tries to neutralise the acid by pouring in water. It is this very neutralisation of the acid that can lead to a remission of pain, a feeling of 'getting better' - until, if the condition is untreated, infection sets in. Yet we still come up against the coincidence factor. It was a very convenient ulcer that perforated Miss Burns' stomach and brought about a miscarriage at a time Angus hoped for one, even though it killed her. Could there have been another factor?

It is possible that she died from an administration of poison. Even here, there is a difficulty in establishing exactly which poison was used. Oil of Savin has such a strong turpentine odour and Oil of Pennyroyal one of mint that we can safely discount them, assuming that the good doctors possessed a sense of smell more highly developed than their sense of justice. One of the weaknesses in the prosecution case, and conversely a strong point in Angus' defence, was never highlighted at the trial, possibly because trials for murder by the administration of corrosive sublimate were outside the experience of most of the participants. It is how on earth Angus ever got Miss Burns to drink a solution of corrosive sublimate in the first place.

When mercury enters the system in the metallic state it is relatively innocuous, but the salts, among which are mercuric nitrate and mercuric cyanide, are all extremely poisonous. Mercuric chloride, or corrosive sublimate, is an intensely violent poison with an acrid and metallic taste. In the very act of swallowing, a painful and burning sensation is experienced in the throat, and this extends all the way down towards the stomach. All the mucous membranes with which the solution comes into contact are attacked and shrivelled. For this reason it has never been a popular weapon of the secret poisoner who must rely on his victim being unaware that poison has been administered. Poisoning by it is much more indicative of accidental swallowing, or suicide.

If Margaret Burns took it herself to get rid of the baby, the agony would have been immediate. It is hardly likely that she drank it during the family breakfast, which is when she was first observed to be ill. Neither did she complain of any pain in her throat. Angus, too, would certainly have known about its effects. As a druggist's assistant he had studied and 'cured' cases of venereal disease, and corrosive sublimate had for years been used for this purpose. Buchan's *Domestic Medicine* supplies a method of giving it. 'One grain of corrosive sublimate is dissolved in two ounces of French Brandy or malt spirits; and of this solution an ordinary tablespoon, or the quantity of half an ounce, is to be taken twice a day, and to be continued as long as any symptoms of the disorder remain'. Even this relatively mild concoction is credited with having a severe effect on the stomach. For those who cannot bear drinking their brandy with such a noxious ingredient, Buchan suggests that the sublimate may be given in the form of a pill.

Every druggist's assistant and apothecary's boy knew how to do this, and it is difficult to imagine Angus trying to administer corrosive sublimate secretly in any other form. Yet how and when did he get Miss Burns to take the pill? No evidence was ever brought forward that on the morning of Wednesday the 23rd of March, Angus gave Miss Burns a pill which shortly after made her violently vomit. She never spoke of it to the servants, or to Angus in the servants' presence. If it was a pill, then the likelihood is it was given with her consent, to cause a miscarriage.

Even here, we stumble over the very root of the mystery. Why would she suddenly agree to it so late in her pregnancy? There was no evidence that she ever took the Oil of Savin or the Oil of Pennyroyal, each of which Angus had at one time in his possession, and both of which would have brought on symptoms indicative of gastrointestinal irritation.

There is no evidence he ever used the instrument on her, which he said was for boring ears, but to which Richardson the cutler assigned a much more sinister purpose. It therefore seems unlikely that whatever she did take she took knowingly. While many of her symptoms certainly suggest poisoning by corrosive sublimate - the three day course of the illness, the violent vomiting, abdominal pain, retention of urine, extreme thirst and difficulty in breathing - when one considers all the other circumstances, it is difficult to imagine corrosive sublimate being the poison used.

If Angus plotted to poison Miss Burns, then he had something else in the house that was just as deadly yet relatively tasteless. Something that was extremely easy to administer without her knowing anything about it. Admittedly, it was mixed in solution with the corrosive sublimate, but when it was mixed was never gone into.

He had arsenic.

Arsenic has an illustrious history. A metallic poison known since ancient times, it has despatched Roman emperors, destroyed princes, and sent to the grave countless spouses. As well as being virtually tasteless it has other qualities which endear it to the secret poisoner - it looks harmless and can easily be made to pass for flour or sugar, and the symptoms it produces, chiefly pain, vomiting and diarrhoea, are characteristic of many ordinary illnesses. When administered in one fatal does, arsenic causes a variety of symptoms which have many features in common with the last days of Margaret Burns. All the signs of intense gastroenteritis develop quite suddenly, and the victim is often prostrated out of sheer physical weakness and exhaustion. Extreme thirst results from the loss of fluid, and suppression of urine and respiratory problems are often experienced. Neurological symptoms are also common, such as weakness in the legs, tingling, numbness and cramps. The vomited material can vary in appearance, and become blackish due to mucus mixed with blood, or greenish due to the presence of bile. The watery diarrhoea often becomes bloody, though this is by no means always the case.

I think that on the balance of probabilities, if poison was administered, it was arsenic and not corrosive sublimate of mercury. I also think that on the balance of probabilities, if Miss Burns died of natural disease, then it was a perforated gastric ulcer that killed her. These two scenarios are not entirely incompatible. It is perfectly feasible that Miss Burns had had a benign gastric ulcer, and a large one at that, for some months prior to her death, and that it was the jolt to her system caused by the administration of arsenic which 'triggered' it off. The irony is that the dose of arsenic need not even have been a fatal one.

There is one final matter to deal with. What can possibly account for Margaret Burns' remarkable 'recovery' on the Friday morning, when the pain and vomiting ceased, and her sudden expiration five hours later while Angus was asleep in his chair? Of all the mysteries in the case, this is perhaps the most taxing. Even if the remission of pain was brought about by water in her body eventually neutralising the acid, a period would have to elapse for toxins to build up and infection to set in. Her sudden recovery and sudden death just do not make any sense, medically speaking. We have reached that stage with the rubik cube when one side just refuses to come out.

There is an answer, and it perhaps goes deeper to the heart of the conspiracy of lies that surrounded the whole affair. To borrow a little from Mark Twain's cynical epigram, it is possible that reports of Miss Burns' recovery were greatly exaggerated. The servants, Betty Nickson and Ann Hopkins, were at great pains during the trial to understate the symptoms, of which they had given a much fuller and more dramatic account at the inquest. Even there it is unlikely that they told the complete truth. It is unimaginable that Margaret Burns could have miscarried, that the baby could have been disposed of, and that the blood could have been cleaned up without them knowing it. So how did Angus obtain their silence?

Let us turn the clock back and try and reconstruct what may have happened. In doing so, we must not lose sight of one important fact. Margaret Burns died in an advanced state of pregnancy shortly before an intended journey to London to seek 'medical advice' from her mother. It is this element which could provide the key to the mystery.

When Miss Burns became pregnant in the late summer of 1807, there was nothing legally to prevent Angus marrying her, though a clergyman might have refused to perform the ceremony. Marriage to a deceased wife's sister was believed by some to be forbidden by Levitical scripture, and consequently frowned upon. (Later that century, such harmless unions would be outlawed by a controversial marriage act). Perhaps Miss Burns wanted to take the legitimate place of Maria in Angus' bed, and was tired of having to conduct their relationship in secret. But Angus neither wanted to marry her, nor raise a fourth child.

Angus wanted Miss Burns to have an abortion, but Miss Burns refused to have one. She wanted to have the child. If she could not be married to him, she would at least have that. Over that winter, as it grew larger in her womb, her determination grew also. Perhaps she did not tell Angus she was pregnant until after the New Year. Angus, shocked at the news, was acutely aware of the scandal that would ensue were he to allow the baby to be born, in light of the amorous activities of his brother Alexander.

Around the middle of February, Angus bought the Oil of Savin from Steele and Oakes the druggists, in the hope that he could still persuade Miss Burns to go through with it. Likewise, a fortnight later he took to be sharpened an instrument, the purpose of which was to insert into the uterus, break the membrane and expel the child. Both of these transactions he carried out in the forlorn hope that even at that late stage he might persuade the stubborn Miss Burns to see sense. This would explain why Angus bought the Oil of Savin and had the instrument sharpened, and yet no evidence was ever brought that he used them. (When examining the Oil of Savin bottle, Steele the druggist said that the Oil of Savin had been replaced by Oil of Pennyroyal. Either Angus did administer the Oil of Savin to her secretly and it had little effect, or Miss Burns poured it away).

Margaret Burns, of course, realised the impropriety and the impossibility of having the baby at Trinity Place, or anywhere else in the port. She therefore made arrangements to travel to London where she expected her mother to accommodate her, and where she might have the baby in relative anonymity. Whether Jane Williams nee McQuistin knew in advance is a matter for speculation. If she did, it would certainly account for a great deal of the ill-feeling between her and Angus over the years that followed, and for her silence at the trial in Angus's defence. It is unlikely that she would have allowed her daughter to have her illegitimate child within the confines of St. James Palace, much more likely that she would have found lodgings somewhere in London for the period of confinement. It would not have been the first time that a young pregnant woman had gone away to have her child, or turned to her mother for help.

Angus knew that the sands of time were running out for him. What Miss Burns' ultimate plans or hopes were it is impossible to say. Whether she stayed in London with her baby and expected him to join her, or whether she intended to return to Liverpool at a later date with the baby in her arms, or to return to Scotland with him, Angus would still have had to support the child at a time when he was struggling to raise his own three. He decides on a drastic measure, to terminate the baby's life before Miss Burns takes herself out of his hands and puts herself into those of her mother. I do not believe that he intended to kill Miss Burns - let us give him the benefit of the doubt on that score. But as he walks back from the Athenaeum on the morning of Wednesday the 23rd of March, he is already contemplating and has already laid the groundwork for his plan.

He has in his possession two deadly poisons, corrosive sublimate of mercury and arsenic. It may already be that a quantity of each is mixed together in solution, but he still possesses each in its unmixed white powder form. Both poisons were widely available then, and Angus would have had no trouble in obtaining them. Corrosive sublimate was in fact freely used as a domestic disinfectant and bug destroyer. He considers the violent effects and unmistakable taste of corrosive sublimate, and wisely selects the arsenic. He is now faced with the problem of how to administer it. We do not know what Miss Burns ate for breakfast, but the Georgian breakfast was a social event in which the family gathered around the table together. Tea and bread were the staples of the meal at the time, the bread buttered and toasted on a fork in front of the fire until the butter melted through it. Marmalade was also a common sight on the breakfast table. The tea would be served with fresh cream which Betty Nickson that morning would have brought from Everton.

The table is set, the participants gathered round. Angus introduces a few grains of arsenic into Miss Burns' tea, not what he considers to be a fatal dose, but enough to cause her illness and, he hopes, a miscarriage. Miss Burns drinks her tea, eats her toast. Breakfast is not a hurried affair. The arsenic has a sudden, dramatic effect. The jolt to her already fragile system causes the large, benign ulcer from which she has suffered to perforate. As the contents flow from her stomach into her abdominal cavity, like sand through a timer, she has now just over fifty hours to live.

After breakfast she lies down on the sofa in the parlour, and the rest of the day she spends in great agony, vomiting and suffering from extreme thirst. Angus tends to her himself. He knows that she dislikes and distrusts doctors and will not readily ask him to send for one. For the rest of that day Angus stays by her side, not leaving the house. He does not know when the baby will come, or indeed if it will come. He cannot stop the servants going about their business. To exclude them from the parlour would be to excite suspicion, and he dare not do that. Perhaps they already suspect that Miss Burns is pregnant and near her full time. Ann Hopkins may only be the cook, but she has been a mother twelve times over.

By Wednesday night, the hoped-for miscarriage has not taken place. Angus determines to sit up with Miss Burns in the parlour, and tells the servants they can go to bed. Miss Burns asks for an easychair to be brought down for Angus, and a quilt and two pillows for herself. Angus now hopes that the hours of darkness will bring the fruits of his, and Miss Burns', labours. But they do not. Thursday dawns and he faces another day of sitting and waiting and hoping. Miss Burns faces a second day of vomiting, raging thirst and great pain. He is tired, he has not slept. Perhaps, he feels, he has miscalculated. Perhaps he should have administered a larger dose. To administer another now might be dangerous. He also has another pressing problem. He dare not allow Miss Burns to suspect that he has poisoned her and is simply hovering like a vulture wait-

ing for the child in her to die. So as soon as the servants enter the parlour on the Thursday morning, Angus takes himself upstairs to bed and
does not come down until breakfast.

Angus has now resigned himself to the fact that if the miscarriage
takes place during the daytime, the servants will have to be a party to the
event. In this he has no choice. He must trust in their complicity and
silence. The clock ticks on. Miss Burns continues to vomit up everything
she is given. Again, to avert any suspicions that Miss Burns might have,
and also to test the loyalty of his servants, he leaves her side and goes to
visit his brother-in-law William Biggam. He knows he is running a risk,
but he is not a great distance away, and he trusts that should it happen in
his absence Betty Nickson will come and fetch him. Besides it is a relief
from having to watch her suffer. He returns about quarter to three in the
afternoon, and finds Miss Burns, he believes, still labouring under simply
the effects of the poison. Perhaps that day there has been talk of bringing in a doctor. But neither of them dare take that chance. Henry Park
would recognise a woman in advanced pregnancy. It must be kept from
the family physician at all costs. Whatever happens over the next few
hours, the secret will be kept within four walls and by four people.

10.00 p.m. Thursday night. 24th of March. Angus prepares to sit
up with Miss Burns for a second night. Once again, he declines the services of the servants. Betty Nickson brings down a clean bedgown for
Miss Burns, and she and Ann Hopkins retire to bed. Perhaps tonight it
will happen. Then, under cover of darkness, Angus can spirit away the
dead child. It is not to happen like that.

1.00 a.m. 2.00 a.m. 3.00 a.m. Miss Burns is breathing heavily,
appears worse. 4.00 a.m. The children are crying in the nursery. Angus
rings the bell once for one of the servants. Betty Nickson leaves the bed
which she shares with Ann Hopkins and comes downstairs, where Angus
asks her to attend the children. While she is up, she can fetch him a jug
of cold water. Betty Nickson sees that Miss Burns is breathing heavily and
seems to be much worse - in fact, the governess is going into labour.
Betty Nickson goes upstairs, tends to the children. By the time she comes
down it is clear that something is wrong. Angus asks her to help him.

Betty Nickson helps Ann Hopkins tie the cloths about her thighs to soak up the blood. A lot of blood soaks into the clean bedgown which Betty Nickson brought down the night before. Miss Burns is in a distraught state, Betty Nickson is frightened, Ann Hopkins who has had twelve children is practical and sympathetic, Angus is relieved that it is all over. Ann Hopkins takes the bloodstained bedgown down into the cellar. Perhaps Miss Burns cradles her dead baby in her arms, reluctant to part with it. Angus tells the servants they can go back to bed. They go, but do not sleep. Sunrise is at six o'clock. Soon it will be getting light.

The servants come back downstairs again shortly after six o'clock. There is maybe blood to clean up in the parlour. They help Miss Burns to dress. She is feeling lighter (naturally) but is still dangerously ill. Perhaps the arsenic has taken its course, but the perforated gastric ulcer has led to peritonitis. The spectre of death is hanging over the house, the fourth time it has called. Thomas McQuistin. Angus' wife, Maria. The baby in Miss Burns' womb. Now Miss Burns herself has just five hours to live.

There is the delicate matter of the disposal of the baby. At his trial, it was implied - though never openly said outright - that Angus got rid of it himself on his way to the Athenaeum. Angus cannot even consider such a course of action. Many of his neighbours in the vicinity of St. Anne Street are also members of the Athenaeum, and he frequently meets with them on his way there. Henry Glover Moore lives at Number 14 and must pass within yards of Trinity Place. They often walk home together in the same direction. A gentleman with a bundle under his arm at that time of the morning would attract unwelcome attention. He cannot risk being seen with such a thing, let alone getting rid of it. And anyway, what if it were found?

A servant girl, however, with a bundle under her arm will invite very little suspicion. Betty Nickson is now prevailed upon to get rid of the baby. Angus tells her that she must go to Everton as usual to fetch the milk and cream for breakfast, and bury the baby on the way. Clearly she cannot take the children on this occasion, so they are kept upstairs in the nursery. Betty Nickson is now providing service over and above the call of duty. She wraps the dead baby in the blood-stained bedgown from the cellar.

With the bundle Betty Nickson leaves the house, furtive at first but then hurrying, turns east towards Soho Street and heads uphill across open countryside towards Everton. It is somewhere here that she buries or conceals the sad, pathetic little bundle. She is still very frightened, and now she runs the rest of the way. This is when she stumbles and sprains her ankle.

Meanwhile, Angus goes to the Athenaeum, believing that he has accomplished his task without causing Miss Burns too prolonged an illness. At the newsroom he shakes hands heartily with Dr. George Coltman, peruses the newspaper, and walks home with the Reverend John Vause. His relief is such that he appears not to be weighed down by worry or to be behaving unnaturally.

The spectre of death is in the house now, waiting. There is nothing any of them can do. Perhaps Miss Burns in the final stages suspects what Angus has done. Betty Nickson has returned from Everton with the milk and cream and a sprained ankle. The poor servant girl is still hysterical. Miss Burns and Ann Hopkins try to calm her down but to no avail. So inconsolable is Betty Nickson that at about ten o'clock Angus resolves to send her for a walk to calm her down. She is told to go to Mr Winstanley's in Henry Street to buy two bottles of wine. So with her sprained ankle and a note, Betty Nickson leaves the house a second time. It is the last time she will see Miss Burns alive.

Ann Hopkins is in the parlour with Angus and Miss Burns. Miss Burns is also very weak from her constant exertions upon the chamber pot, and obviously very distressed following her miscarriage. Still fulfilling her role as housekeeper, she orders dinner, perhaps more for Angus than herself. One cannot imagine Miss Burns feels like eating. About a pint of thin gruel and some warm beer are all she has managed that morning. Ann Hopkins leaves the parlour and goes downstairs to the kitchen. It is the last time the cook will see Miss Burns alive.

Angus is exhausted. He has hardly slept for two nights. He sits in his easychair and falls into a deep sleep. Miss Burns has such terrible pain in her abdomen and needs to use the chamber pot again. She has not the heart to wake Angus from the deep satisfying sleep into which he has fallen. She stands up from the sofa, picks up the chamber pot, intending to go into the other parlour. She finds that it is impossible for her to stand. She makes it as far as the door, where she collapses, dropping the chamber pot. She is too weak even to call out. She tries to crawl back to the sofa, but does not make it. She rests in the corner, against the wall, and there she remains for the last moments of her life. While Angus sleeps, death reaches out and wraps her in its cold embrace.

(Much suspicion was heaped upon Angus' being asleep at this time. I am inclined to believe that of the story the servants told, this at least was true. If Angus had been awake when Miss Burns collapsed, he would surely have helped her back onto the sofa, and rung for Ann Hopkins. For all his faults, it seems strangely out of character that he should leave her in such an ungraceful position on the floor and then pretend to be asleep).

Miss Burns has been dead only minutes when Betty Nickson comes back into the parlour with the wine. She and Ann Hopkins wake Angus and have to shake him out of his deep sleep. He is genuinely distressed to find Miss Burns dead and knows that he is responsible for it. Betty runs (or rather hobbles) to fetch Angus' sister and brother-in-law, the Biggams, and they collect Miss Burns' friend from Hunter Street, Elizabeth Jones, on the way.

There is no secret any more that she was pregnant, and that she has had a baby. Everyone can see the state she has died in. The only secret is how she met her death. Nobody fetches a doctor. It is hoped that by the time a doctor comes, the swelling will have gone down. Maybe they press on her. One thing is clear. They are doing it for Angus' sake, to shield and protect him from the scandal that might ensue. Angus has enemies in Liverpool, but he also has friends.

Conspiracies of silence are rarely thought out and planned. The participants in such a conspiracy all have their individual and separate reasons for keeping quite. The Biggams because they are family. Elizabeth Jones because she has perhaps known all along that her friend was pregnant, and kept it a secret. The servants because they are already part of it. At some point, Angus lectures the servants on the need for them to say nothing about what has happened. He talks about the goodness of Miss Burns to him and the children. The children. They are part of all this. Their father must not be disgraced or charged with anything for their sake.

And just in case anyone ever suspects, Angus takes what is left of the arsenic and mixes it in solution with the corrosive sublimate. Jacob's Water. Stuff to poison the moths with. But wait. The best trick is yet to come. He labels another bottle. He writes on the label Poison Water, and transfers the solution into that. He then fills up the Jacob's Water bottles with something innocuous. What better defence has he than a bottle of poison, clearly labelled as poison, in a place to which Miss Burns had access - his own medicine chest. It is a masterly stroke. To conceal something by placing it where it can be plainly seen. (This would explain why Dr. Bostock found nothing of a poisonous nature in the Jacob's Water bottles, although Jane Overhin and Elizabeth Jones both testified that Jacob's Water was the stuff Angus used to poison the moths.)

Of course there is always a risk that at the inquest one or both of the servants will tell the truth and shame the devil. What stops them doing so are the rumours circulating that Angus has poisoned Miss Burns. They have no desire to be part of that, for that is murder. And their silence becomes set in stone. Nearer the trial, the prosecution authorities pick on the wrong servant for aiding and abetting, fasten on the wrong poison, and link the wrong person with the disposal of the child. There is not much they get right.

We shall never know for certain. But that is the perennial delight of mysteries. The crime with which Angus was charged was not an extraordinary or unusual one. Unwanted children have been behind many murders. From Georgian times to the present day, the criminal calender reveals many mundane instances. Angus may have been whiter or blacker than I have painted. The rubik cube may be twisted this way and that. I have attempted to give him the benefit of the doubt, and come up with a verdict of manslaughter. The death of the baby is, of course, another matter.

Only one thing can be said with complete certainty. He was lucky to escape the gallows. Were he to have been tried in his native Scotland, a verdict of Not Proven would have been available to the jury. Let us avail ourselves of that verdict and conclude that his acquittal at Lancaster was the only outcome demanded by justice, and the best thing that could have happened under the circumstances.

POSTSCRIPT

In its day, the Angus case excited as much controversy and captured as much attention as the murder of James Maybrick, the Liverpool cotton merchant, now ludicrously presented as Jack the Ripper, eighty-one years later. Florence Maybrick, his American-born wife, was convicted – many thought unfairly – of poisoning him with arsenic. She was tried at St. George's Hall, that magnificent edifice which now stands in the area vacated by the old Royal Infirmary and Seamen's Hospital past which Angus would have walked on his way to the Athenaeum.

The Liverpool that Charles Angus knew no longer exists. From where Trinity Place used to be, one has to walk a very long way indeed to reach open countryside. St. Anne Street is a symbol of inner city decay, its mansions and fine gardens long gone. The crème de la crème of Liverpool society who once lived there, if they could return briefly, would walk by without a glance. With a little imagination one can still look up the hill towards Everton and ponder on past crimes.

If Angus were to come back, and try to retrace his steps to the newsroom, he would find nothing that was familiar. Church Street is now part of a large shopping precinct, so redolent of many city centres. The old Athenaeum has gone, but the institution still exists in a narrow road off called Church Alley. If Angus could find the door and enter, he would recognise a few furnishings - a bureau, the chandelier over the staircase. Many of the volumes were there in Angus' time. So is the book in which his membership is recorded, along with his resignation. It is still a haven of learning in a city which has never embraced culture as much as commerce.

Travellers now journey across the Atlantic in a matter of hours rather than weeks. Four miles east of Moneague on the main A3 road to

Kingston, Jamaica, one comes to St. Faith's Penn, a gastronomic halt on a tour of the island. A dozen or more stalls offer such tempting delicacies as roasted yam with a sliver of salt fish roasted in the embers, ripe bananas, boiled corn on the cob, and when they are in season, sweet sops and avocado pears. The gourmet may also tickle his palate with cow pod soup, which locals will tell you increases the procreative powers. It is, they say, full of bull. In that humble culinary item, colloquially speaking, the spirit of Angus' brother William lives on.

To taste and smell the world that Charles Angus knew one has to travel to Scotland, and explore the twisting rural byways of the Mull of Galloway. Curghie, where he stayed for a number of years after his trial, is a blink-and-you-miss-it place. The road doesn't go much further, curling round a crooked green finger of land that terminates at the Mull of Galloway lighthouse. Fulmar nest in the high cliffs, taking off to soar and wheel above an ocean that seems to boil like the surface of a cauldron. It is not hard to picture Angus walking here, shooting at seabirds with the gun he once kept in readiness against Napoleon.

Alternatively one can drive northwards from Stranraer, Angus' birthplace, up the coast towards Ballantrae and Turnberry. It is a romantic coastline, graced with romantic names, from which the island of Ailsa Craig never looks more haunting than in an evening twilight. Just after it crosses the Galloway border into Ayrshire, the road climbs eastward up the edge of Glen App. A single track road, easy to miss, goes off to the left and crosses the river by an old, arched stone bridge before heading up past dense thickets and rhododendron bushes into the heart of that most reclusive of Scottish glens. Finart House, which Angus rented and lived in after his trial, and where his brother Alexander died, was demolished in the 1940's. Nettles smother the foundations but cannot hide the resilient fragments of garden wall that cling on, testament to the fact that there was once a house here. It was a fine house too. Jenny McClung, who lives in Ballantrae, used to be a tablemaid there in the 1920s. She told me that there were rumours of a secret tunnel that ran from beneath the house to the bay, though she never found it. When the house was demolished, the turret above the smokeroom was discovered to be full of ancient honeycombs, blackened by time and smoke. If there are ghosts, they walk here.

Turnberry Lodge, where Angus died, still stands. It is an unusual house in the gothic style, still recognisable from two drawings which Angus' daughter Maria made of it in her sketchbook. Dairy farmer Billy Gray has lived in the house all his life. One wet August Sunday, he and his wife Pat invited me to take lunch there, and while the rain blotted out the surrounding fields, I sat in front of a blazing log fire and held a glass of wine where Angus must have downed many an after-dinner tipple. How he came to depart life at the age of fifty-three must remain a mystery. Perhaps he perished of consumption, the disease, all too common at the time, which carried off his child bride many years before. There are no ghosts at Turnberry Lodge. One can only hope that, after an eventful and dramatic life, whatever secrets he took to his grave, he took peacefully.

A mile or so inland across the green, windswept slopes, that grave can still be seen in the old kirkyard of Kirkoswald, the tall stone and its proud inscription mute testimony that he did not die unloved and unmourned. It has weathered well considering the Scottish climate, but the letters are crumbling now as ivy spreads up and over them, no respecter of things or persons past. A separate block of granite has been placed at its base, like a death's visiting book, recording the names of all who enter. Six people lie buried here - Angus, his daughter Jane, his son Thomas, his son-in-law, and two grandchildren, one of whom ended his days in Clinton Furnace, Kentucky.

The neatly kept kirkyard has a serene air, except on summer weekends when charabancs of tourists stop to pay homage. Yet it is not Angus' grave they come to see. That stands largely forgotten and ignored, even though it is only yards from where they step. The fame of Kirkoswald rests with it being the village where the poet Robert Burns went to school in the summer of 1775. Burns' schoolmaster, Hugh Rodger, is buried close by, as are the poet's grand and great-grandparents on his mother's side. The earth has also consumed three people immortalised in Burns' famous poem *Tam O'Shanter* - Jean Kennedy, John Davidson, and Douglas Graham, the 'Kirkton Jean', 'Souter Johnnie' and 'Tam' himself, who on his nightmare gallop home, pursued by warlocks and witches, his belly fully of ale, spied upon an altar 'a murderer's banes, in gibbet-airns; twa span-lang wee unchristened bairns'.

It is deeply ironic that even in death the names of Angus and Burns are joined for all time.

ACKNOWLEDGEMENTS

This is the first book on the Angus/Burns case and all material used is from primary sources. It could not have been written without the help of numerous libraries, organisations and individuals. My grateful thanks go to the staff who helped me in the Picton Library, Liverpool; Blackburn and Clitheroe Public Libraries; Lancaster Public Library; Ayr Public Library; The Guildhall Library, London; Lincoln's Inn Library and the Inner Temple Library, London; the Liverpool Medical Institution; the Liverpool Athenaeum; the Lancashire Record Office, Preston; the Family Centre of the Church of Jesus Christ of Latter Day Saints, Kensington, London; Eton College Archives; the Chester Record Office; Lancaster Castle; the Scottish Records Office; the General Register Office (Scotland); Edinburgh University Library (Special Collections); The Royal College of Surgeons, Edinburgh; Stranraer Museum and the Wigtown Free Press.

My special thanks go to Mrs Samuels of the Liverpool Medical Institution for 'ferreting' about for me, and with whose kind and always prompt help I was able to immerse myself in the medical history of Liverpool; Donny Nelson of the Wigtown Free Press in Stranraer; Marion Frearson for her advice on genealogical matters; Jenny McClung and Billy King of Ballantrae; Billy and Pat Gray of Turnberry; Alan Clark for searching old graveyards with me, and taking photographs; Chris Delaney for reading the manuscript as it progressed, making helpful suggestions, and for assistance with the map of Angus' Liverpool; Keith Skinner, for tips on research; Mr John S.G. Blair, President of the Scottish Society for the History of Medicine; to Richard Whittington-Egan, friend and mentor, who told me to stop thinking about writing an Angus book and do it, and who kindly provided a foreword in his inimitable style; and to my agent, Diana Tyler, for more than words can say.

Incalculable is the only word to describe the debt of gratitude I owe to Peter F.H. Robson, Charles Angus' great great great grandson, and a keen family historian, who gave me unlimited access to material in his possession, including Angus' letter book and family correspondence of the period. However cliched it might sound, without the help of Peter and other Angus family descendants who retained and passed on historic artifacts over the centuries, this book could never have been written. I owe a great deal to the American descendants of Charles Angus, particularly Alexander McDermott of Los Angeles, for permission to use the Angus family portraits in this book.

For the use of the photographs of the Angus family portraits, my thanks go to Max Payne, Photographic Artist, Coldyhill Lane, Newby, Scarborough, and for much hospitality and friendship on my many visits to their home, I would like to say a special thank you to Peter's wife, Ruth Robson.

Finally, for assistance with the medical aspects of the case, I should like to express my gratitude to the Scottish Poisons Unit, to Dr Ian R. Hill, OBE, MA, MD, PhD, MRC path, Consultant Forensic Pathologist, Dept. of Forensic Medicine, Guys Hospital, London, and to Mr John P.S. Cochrane, MS, FRCS, Consultant Surgeon. The last-named, particularly, gave up much valuable time to help me try and solve the complex medical puzzles raised by the curious death of Margaret Burns.

Notes on Sources

For information on the history of Liverpool and many of its char-
acters, I am indebted to the following publications:

Memorials of Liverpool Sir James Picton 1907

Liverpool as it was during the Last Quarter
of the Eighteenth Century Richard Brook F.S.A. 1853

Liverpool a Few Years Since An Old Stager 1885

Recollections of Old Liverpool J. Stonehouse 1863

The Medical History of Liverpool F.D. Fletcher

An address to the Governors of Liverpool
Dispensary: containing a defence of the
resolution of the late General Meeting, to
increase the number of the Medical Officers
to that Institution Dr. James Carson 1805

Liverpool, Capital of the Slave Trade
Gail Cameron and Stan Crooke 1992

For matters relating to the trial and its aftermath, I used:

The Trial of Charles Angus
Taken in shorthand by William Jones, June 1808

*A Vindication of the Opinions delivered in
Evidence by the Medical Witnesses for the
Crown on a late trial at Lancaster for murder*
Dr. Rutter, Dr. Gerard, Dr. Bostock and
Thomas Fairfax Hay 1808

*Remarks on a late publication entitled
'A Vindication . . . etc'* Dr. James Carson 1808

*Exposure of some of the false statements
contained in Dr. Carson's pamphlet
entitled 'Remarks . . . etc'* in a letter
addressed to that gentleman J. Dawson 1809

*Reflections occasioned by the perusal of a
pamphlet entitled 'A Vindication . . . etc'*
D. Campbell 1809

For a comprehensive and richly detailed account of British
Slavery I consulted:

Black Ivory James Walvin 1992

All information and correspondence regarding Angus' slave-trading adventures, and family matters, are taken from the personal archives of Peter F.H. Robson.

Index

Although not referred to by name in the text, the jury at the trial of Charles Angus at the Lancaster Assizes were Thomas Briggs, John Jackson, John Strickland, James Roberts, Thomas Clark, Thomas Burrow, John Greenwood, William Hargreaves, Richard Hartley, John Fawcett, Thomas Thornbull, Thomas Wilkinson.